CROSS✦ROADS

PRAYER

Author
Richard J. Reichert

**BROWN-ROA**
A Division of Harcourt Brace & Company

BROWN-ROA

A Division of Harcourt Brace & Company

O u r   M i s s i o n

The primary mission of BROWN-ROA is to provide the
Catholic and Christian educational markets with the
highest quality catechetical print and media resources.
The content of these resources reflects the best insights
of current theology, methodology, and pedagogical research.
The resources are practical and easy to use, designed to meet
expressed market needs, and written to reflect the
teachings of the Catholic Church.

Nihil Obstat
Rev. Richard L. Schaefer
Imprimatur
✠ Most Rev. Jerome Hanus, O.S.B.
Archbishop of Dubuque
January 4, 1998
Feast of St. Elizabeth Ann Seton

The Imprimatur is an official declaration that a book or pamphlet is free of doctrinal or moral error. No
implication is contained therein that anyone who granted the Imprimatur agrees with the contents, opinions,
or statements expressed.

Photo Credits
Nancy Anne Dawe—41, 89; Mimi Forsyth—56, 91, 92, 94–95; Robert Cushman Hayes—4;
Gene Plaisted, OSC/CROSIERS—73, 80; James L. Shaffer—17, 46, 75; Skjold Photography—8, 19,
32, 35, 37, 50, 55b, 60, 67, 69; D. Jeanene Tiner—44, 55t; Jim Whitmer—23

Printed in the United States of America

ISBN 0-15-950464-3

10 9 8 7 6 5 4 3 2 1

Here are the Questions. Where Are the Answers?

May We Have a Moment of Your Time?

Center for Religious Trends
4040 Crossroads Boulevard
Dorr, Kansas 03514
(888) 555-1240

Dear Young Person:

We at the Center for Religious Trends are interested in you! The Center is a research group interested in learning more about the religious practices of young people. We are asking persons ages 12–17 in the United States to fill out the following questionnaire. The group is looking for religious trends among teens in various areas of the country. You need not sign your name on the questionnaire; your responses will be kept confidential, used only for scientific research. We anxiously await your reply. Thank you for your time!

Instructions: Using an ink pen, complete the following statements. Check as many responses for each question as appropriate.

How often do you pray?
- ❑ 9 + times a day
- ❑ 6–8 times a day
- ❑ 3–5 times a day
- ❑ 1–2 times a day
- ❑ I don't pray.

At what time during the day do you pray?
- ❑ In the morning
- ❑ Before meals
- ❑ In the afternoon
- ❑ In the evening
- ❑ Before I go to sleep
- ❑ Other: _____

Where do you pray?
- ❑ At the table
- ❑ In church
- ❑ In bed
- ❑ In the car or on the bus
- ❑ Everywhere
- ❑ Other: _____

What method of prayer do you use?
- ❑ Talking to God
- ❑ Saying formal prayers
- ❑ Singing
- ❑ Dancing
- ❑ Other: _____

Why do you pray?
- ❑ For guidance
- ❑ For others
- ❑ For help during a crisis
- ❑ To ask forgiveness
- ❑ To give thanks
- ❑ Other: _____

Please define prayer in your own words (one hundred words or less).

_____
_____
_____
_____
_____
_____
_____

Thank you for participating in our study!

Who Will Listen to Me?

☇ *Read the signs* 🎬

The following are some past and present symbols and crosses of the Christian Church. Try to match each symbol with the description of what it represents.

_____ Symbol of prayer.

_____ Originating in the fifteenth century, this symbolizes the innocence of the Baby Jesus.

_____ Symbol used secretly in the catacombs by the persecuted Christians to let others know that they, too, were followers of Jesus.

_____ God is the beginning, continuation, and the end of all things.

_____ Used in the catacombs, this symbolizes the loving care of Jesus.

_____ It is believed that this cross was taken from what we now know as Ireland to the island of Iona by Columba in the sixth century.

_____ Symbol of the faithful feeding on the blood of Christ.

_____ Originating in ancient Egypt, this cross was used by the early Christians in the catacombs.

_____ Since ancient times, this has symbolized love.

_____ Symbol of Mary, selected by the French kings as their symbol and used in the banner of Joan of Arc.

Religion past and present

Religion has been around a long time. Anthropologists (those who study the science of human beings, especially their origin, nature, and destiny) have found solid evidence of religious practices dating back to 60,000 B.C.E. But experts believe that religion has been around longer than that. When do you think religion first appeared in society?

150,000 years ago	500,000 years ago	1,000,000 years ago	2,000,000 years ago

Circle your response, and you will find the answer later in this section.

There are thousands of religions in the world today. Despite the great differences between religions, there is one characteristic common in most religions, past and present —the practice of prayer.

Within the many religions, there is a great amount of variety in prayer—including the way people pray, the times people pray, what they pray for, where they pray, and to whom they pray. Why people have always prayed is simple: The people believed in the existence of a god or multiple gods whose help they needed on earth. How people have prayed throughout the centuries depended on who they believed their god or gods to be.

Prehistoric peoples believed in good and evil spirits and powers. The good spirits provided the things the people benefited from, such as plants and animals. The evil spirits were responsible for the things that could harm the people, such as earthquakes and floods. These people established rituals, prayers, and ceremonies to keep the good spirits happy and to drive off the evil spirits.

A Prayer Tradition ✛

The Chinese use firecrackers as a form of prayer intended to ward off evil spirits.

The ancient Greeks and Romans believed in an entire community of gods and goddesses, each with human qualities, a distinct personality, and a particular position in life. The people would pray to these gods and goddesses for favors and blessings.

Stories or myths were created to explain certain events in life. For example, the changing of the seasons was attributed to Demeter, the Greek goddess of corn, grain, and the harvest. Demeter's daughter Persephone was abducted by Hades, the god of the underworld, who wanted Persephone to be his wife. Demeter was so upset at the loss of her daughter that she put a curse on the world that caused all the plants to die. Zeus, the supreme ruler of the gods, became alarmed at the curse and sought for the return of Persephone. But Hades had control over Persephone simply because she had eaten while in the underworld. Finally it was decided that Persephone would spend four months of the year in the underworld. During this time, Demeter grieved so greatly for her daughter that she took back her gifts to the world—the corn, the grain, and the harvest. This time without any plants and crops is known as winter. When Persephone was returned, Demeter graced the land with her gifts once again, thus the beginning of spring.

Activity

The following is a list of gods and goddesses ancient Greeks and Romans worshiped. Try your best to match each Greek god or goddess with his or her position and his or her Roman counterpart.

Greek	Position	Roman
Aphrodite	god of commerce and science	Apollo
Apollo	god of fire and metalworking	Bacchus
Ares	god of light, medicine, and poetry	Ceres
Artemis	god of love	Cupid
Athena	god of sleep	Diana
Demeter	god of the sea	Jupiter
Dionysus	god of war	Mars
Eros	god of wine and fertility	Mercury
Hephaestus	goddess of crafts, war, wisdom	Minerva
Hermes	goddess of growing things	Neptune
Hypnos	goddess of hunting and childbirth	Somnus
Poseidon	goddess of love	Venus
Zeus	ruler of the gods	Vulcan

Can you think of any words in the English language we use today that derive from the names of Greek and Roman gods and goddesses? For instance, the word *panic* comes from the name of the Greek god of pastures, flocks, and shepherds—*Pan*. It was believed that Pan created noises in the woods at night that frightened and scared travelers; they were in a state of panic.

For starters, see what you can find in the dictionary under the word *nemesis*.

In the fifteenth and sixteenth centuries, the Incas ruled a vast empire in South America. Religion was an important part of their daily life. They, too, believed in numerous gods and goddesses, the most important one being Viracocha, the god that created nature. An important part of their religious ceremonies were sacrifices and offerings to the gods and goddesses. Crops and animals, such as llamas, were offered to keep the gods happy, so that they would not take vengeance on the people. In certain instances, human sacrifices were made. This was not a punishment for the sacrificed person but rather an honor.

So how long do you think religion has existed? Experts believe that religion has played an important role in society from the time humans first appeared on earth—approximately *two million years ago*!

How do you define "prayer"?

_____

_____

_____

The many faces of God

As time has changed, so has our understanding of God. Through God's self-revelation in the Old Testament and through the gift of faith, we now know how loving, gracious, and compassionate God is. In fact, many of the images of God we use today describe these qualities, such as the Gentle One, the Giver of Gifts, the Forgiving One. The following is a list of some of the qualities of God revealed to us:

- God is like a loving parent who regards each of us as beloved children.

- God is always near, always available to us; God is eager to be with us.

- God is personally concerned about what is going on in our lives.

- God is eager for us to be happy and to experience the fullness of life.

- God is infinitely patient with our shortcomings.

- God is infinitely merciful, always ready and eager to forgive us whenever we turn to God in sorrow.

- God is faithful and will never go back on the promises made to us.

- God is all-powerful, the Creator of all things and in total control of that creation.

- God is eager to continue to communicate with us, enlighten us, guide us, and share God's wisdom with us as we journey through life.

If you really believe God is all these things (and much more, of course)—a loving, doting parent, an intimate friend, your protector and your guide—that belief will shape both *why you pray* and *how you pray.*

How do you imagine God?

_____
_____
_____

Prayer is . . .

With this understanding of God, we can begin to look at how the Church views prayer. Perhaps the best definition of prayer you'll find in our Church's tradition is this very simple one: *Prayer is raising your mind and heart to God.* Let's examine this definition more closely.

Prayer is raising your mind and heart to God. The act of raising simply means that you need to direct your attention toward God. Raising your mind and heart to God tells us that praying should involve and engage your whole person—your thoughts and your feelings, your ideas and your love.

In what type of situations do you give your full attention, sharing your thoughts and feelings, your ideas and love?

What do you do?

You've noticed your friend has been withdrawn lately, not wanting to come to your house, to go swimming, or to go to the movies. In fact, she has missed several days of school in the last few weeks. You are very concerned about her. What do you do?

_____

_____

_____

_____

Your best friend wants to sit down with you to have a heart-to-heart talk. He needs to tell you something very important that he has not shared with anyone else. Your friend just found out he is HIV-positive. What do you do?

_____

_____

_____

_____

One of your classmates comes to school with a black eye. She says she was accidentally hit in the face while playing baseball. But this isn't the first time she has come to school bruised and battered. Three weeks ago she "fell" down the stairs and sprained her wrist. You have a feeling these events were not accidents. What do you do?

_____

_____

_____

_____

_____

When you stop and think about it, you naturally or instinctively share your thoughts and feelings, ideas and love, any time you really want to communicate or to get in touch with someone. Through heart-to-heart conversations, you open and share your heart (as well as your mind) with those you love. But communication is a two-way street. You must pay attention and listen to the conversation closely. Only then can you offer straight-from-the-heart advice, encouragement, love, and support.

If your best friend came to your house upset and crying, you would probably want to sit down together and talk. You may go upstairs to your bedroom, put away your homework or shut down the computer, turn off the CD player, and close the door. You want to focus your full attention on your friend. You tell your friend not just what you think; you also communicate how you feel. You share your thoughts and feelings, ideas and love, with your friend. You raise your mind and your heart to your friend.

God, too, is a dear friend. With his grace, God calls us to respond to his offer of friendship. So prayer is simply a conversation with God, just like any talk with a close friend. You focus your full attention on God, free of distractions and interruptions. Then you share your whole self with God, your mind and your heart. But you must also listen to God. You must open your mind and your heart to what God wants to share with you.

"And whenever you pray, do not be like the hypocrites; for they love to stand and pray in the synagogues and at the street corners, so that they may be seen by others. Truly I tell you, they have received their reward. But whenever you pray, go into your room and shut the door and pray to your Father who is in secret; and your Father who sees in secret will reward you.

"When you are praying, do not heap up empty phrases as the Gentiles do; for they think that they will be heard because of their many words. Do not be like them, for your Father knows what you need before you ask him."

—Matthew 6:5–8

How do you feel you could improve your prayer life and make your faith experiences more meaningful?

_____

_____

_____

A Prayer Tradition ✦

Five times each day devout Muslims stop whatever they are doing, turn toward Mecca, kneel with their forehead touching the ground, and offer prayers to Allah. They chant, "There is no God but Allah, and Muhammad is His Prophet!" The five times in the day when Muslims pray are when they rise from bed in the morning, at noon (when the sun is overhead), in the mid-afternoon, at sunset, and before bed.

A lifelong friend

Suppose four people in four different countries of the world—Peru, Kenya, India, and Russia—started traveling north. Eventually, they would meet at the same point—the North Pole. Prayer is something like that. Different people have different ways of praying. But if they pray long enough, they all end with the same result—a closer, more intimate relationship with God.

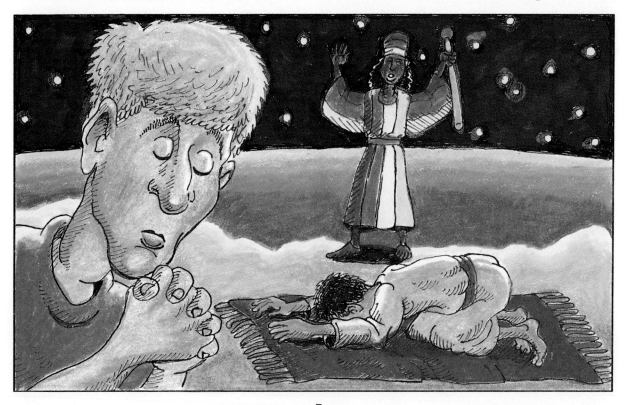

You see, the core of all prayer is communication with God. From communication comes communion, a special sharing with God. Whenever you focus your attention on another person, share your thoughts and feelings with that person, and strive to be open to what the other person is sharing with you, you form a close bond with that person. You become more united in thoughts and feelings. You grow in shared trust and affection for each other.

As you'll see, prayer can take many different forms. At different times you may have different reasons for praying. That doesn't matter. Whether you pray aloud or silently, alone or with others, praying still involves communicating with God. Whether you are moved to pray out of need, out of gratitude, or out of sorrow, you are still communicating with God. And communicating with God always leads to communion with God.

Catechism Key

. . . The grace of the Kingdom is "the union of the entire holy and royal Trinity . . . with the whole human spirit." [St. Gregory of Nazianzus, Oratio, 16, 9: PG 35, 945.] Thus, the life of prayer is the habit of being in the presence of the thrice-holy God and in communion with him. . . . (2565)

Describe your best friend and your relationship with him or her. What qualities make your best friend so special? What qualities make you a good friend? What makes good friendships last?

_____

_____

_____

_____

_____

"Being tight" with God

Sometimes we describe two close friends by saying they are "really tight." "Being tight" means that two friends enjoy spending time together and are there for each other in times of need. They have the same interests and enjoy the same activities. There are no secrets between the two. "Being tight" with someone is a way of describing all that goes into a close, intimate friendship.

As your friend, God wants to be "tight" with you! Review once more the list on page four of some of the qualities of God revealed to us. Do any of these qualities suggest that God wants you to keep your distance? Do any of them suggest that God is unapproachable? It's just the opposite, isn't it?

Recall the life and words of Jesus, the Son of God and God's fullest revelation to us. Jesus is gentle, humble, forgiving, caring. Jesus is always available, always reaching out, always inviting his followers to closer friendship.

That's exactly how we should think of God when we pray. Sure God is totally awesome, all-powerful, the Supreme Being. But God is also extremely approachable, gentle, concerned about you. Reaching out with open arms, God is truly eager to be best friends with you. So when we talk about prayer leading to communion with God, we're talking about real intimacy, a deep, personal friendship. That's the true goal and the ultimate effect of all prayer. After all, prayer is communication, and communication leads to communion—"being tight"—with God.

A Prayer Tradition ✦

The followers of Sufism, a division of the religion of Islam, practice a sacred dance. In this dance, they spin around rapidly until they enter a trance, through which they hope to experience a divine presence.

Hello God; are you there?

Sure, praying sounds easy, but how do you focus your attention on something that isn't visible, something that you can't see or hear? How can you be sure you are praying and not just talking to yourself? Do you ever see any results of your prayer?

Prayer may be more difficult than it seems at first. It can be tough trying to establish intimacy or communion with an invisible being, much less a special friendship. When you pray in a group, such as during Mass, you are expected to say words you may not understand or that may not exactly express what you want to say. Finally, after all your prayers have been said, it may still seem that prayer simply doesn't work. At some time, you have probably asked God for help or for a favor and didn't see any response.

Besides, praying takes time, and it may seem you don't have a lot of free time.

You've got homework, household chores, school activities, and sports. When you do have free time, you'd rather do more fun things, such as playing Nintendo or surfing the Internet. It's more fun hanging out with friends you can see and hear than it is talking to a God you can't see or hear.

Given all these real problems, it's no surprise that you—and many other people your age—may not find the idea of developing a prayer life too exciting or appealing. But don't worry. None of these problems are so big you can't overcome them.

A Prayer Tradition ✦

Hindus use mechanical aids such as prayer wheels to pray. They write prayers on little wheels that are then turned either by water or wind. Each time the wheel turns, they believe a prayer is said, even if they are not around to see the wheel turn.

A basis for prayer

Even if developing a prayer life seems like a big challenge, keep in mind that you already have a lot going for you. **First,** if you are honest, you really do want to get in touch with God. Every person has a basic instinct or desire for closeness with God. This is God's grace, calling us to union with God. Also, every person knows that this relationship can't be developed alone; you need God— God's care, support, help, and love.

Second, despite the real problems of trying to relate to a God who is invisible, "talking with God" is actually a very simple process. If you can talk, you can talk with God. If you can listen, you can learn to hear God. You come equipped with all it takes to pray. Praying doesn't involve any special talents or abilities you need to acquire. You may lack the natural talent needed to play the piano. You may lack the natural talent needed to be a professional athlete. You may never be a whiz at math. But you do have the natural ability to pray. All you need to do is exercise and develop this talent. And like any natural talent, the more you develop it, the easier it gets to use it. Once you get the hang of it and it becomes a regular part of your life, prayer is something you don't forget how to do—just like riding a bicycle.

Third, and most important, God is even more eager to communicate and enter into communion with you than you may be to communicate and enter into communion with God. In other words, you can expect God to take the initiative, to reach out, to invite, to encourage and help you grow in your ability to pray.

When it comes to developing a prayer life, you definitely aren't alone. Not only do you have the love and guidance of God, but you also have the support of your faith community—the Church—helping you grow in prayer. Prayer and Christian life are inseparable. You have everything needed to develop a meaningful prayer life. Are you ready?

Catechism Key

"If you knew the gift of God!" [Jn 4:10.] The wonder of prayer is revealed beside the well where we come seeking water: there, Christ comes to meet every human being. It is he who first seeks us and asks us for a drink. Jesus thirsts; his asking arises from the depths of God's desire for us. Whether we realize it or not, prayer is the encounter of God's thirst with ours. God thirsts that we may thirst for him. [Cf. St. Augustine, De diversis quaestionibus octoginta tribus 64, 4: PL 40, 56.] (2560)

Pause to Pray

*God of compassion and tenderness,
lover of people,
friend of the poor,
be my friend and love me tenderly.
Be with me every moment of my day,
be in my sleepy eyes as I awake,
smile at me from my morning mirror,
share my breakfast with me, Lord.
Be with me every moment of my day,
be on the lips of those who speak to me,
and in my ears as I listen to them talk.
Be with me every moment of my day,
be with me as I end this day,
and search for sleep and quiet repose,
be with me in my dreams both good and bad
that I may arise eager and ready
to spend another day with you.
Amen.*

—*Excerpt from* Prayer-talk *by
William V. Coleman
(Notre Dame, IN: Ave Maria Press, 1983),
page 86.*

God: I really have to smile at some of my children.

Me: Why, God?

God: Today I listened to a long prayer from a very good man (at least he and others hold him in high esteem). For a full 30 minutes he explained to me just what he wanted done and how to do it. He is a school principal and sounded as if he were speaking to one of his first grade students.

Me: Are you insulted, God?

God: No, no, not at all. I know my children well. I understand how nervous and even frantic they get. I realize that their hearts are in the right place, but I still have to smile—talking to God as if he were a first grader. It is no more than an occupational hazard of being principal. He talks to his wife that way, too.

Me: How should we pray, God?

God: You don't remember?

Me: What Jesus said? The Our Father?

God: That's the model. All your prayers should sound like that one. Notice that the beginning of the prayer is all about me, then it focuses on you. All prayers should have that kind of balance.

Me: I always get so interested in the me part of it that I forget to talk about you. It's not that I am selfish, God. I think, though, that I get so zeroed in on mentioning special requests that I forget that I should be saying a few nice things to you, too.

God: Please remember that. It is not that I need to hear them; you need to say them. Otherwise you make our relationship like a cafeteria. You come in and go through the line and pick out a bit of this and a bit of that. Meanwhile you forget who is providing the food.

—Excerpt from Prayer-talk *by William V. Coleman (Notre Dame, IN: Ave Maria Press, 1983), pages 84–85.*

Homework

The following is a basic outline of how many Catholic prayers are composed.

1. **YOU:** The prayer begins by addressing God with an appropriate title or name.

2. **WHO:** Next, the prayer recalls some past deeds or actions of God.

3. **DO:** The prayer then states what is being asked of God.

4. **THROUGH:** Lastly, the prayer ends by offering the prayer through Jesus, our High Priest.

All merciful God,

who led your people out of slavery in the land of Egypt to the freedom of the Promised Land,

please free us of the prejudice and fear that hold us captive.

We ask this through Jesus, your only Son and our Savior.

Use this formula to compose a personal prayer expressing an interest, need, or concern you have right now.

[**You**] _____ ,

[**Who**] _____

[**Do**] _____

[**Through**] _____

Extra! Extra!

In your own words and with your own thoughts and feelings, please answer the title of this chapter: Who will listen to me? Your answer should be a paragraph of fifty words or more. Write your answer on page 99 of the appendix.

What Should I Say?

 Feature Story

Suppose a reporter from *Teen Age* magazine called and said she wanted to do a feature article on YOU! She asks you to prepare a list of topics she can discuss with you when she does the interview. Possible topics include your hopes and dreams, your fears, recent successes and failures, your friends, your school life, interests and hobbies, and your family. What are eight topics you would put on the list? Give a reason for each topic as to why you would want to discuss that topic.

1.

2.

3.

4.

5.

6.

7.

8.

A message for every occasion

Stores usually display their greeting cards in sections according to specific topics, such as Birthday, Get Well, Congratulations, Thank You, Thinking of You, and Sympathy, not to mention the holiday-of-the-month. Just by browsing in the store you know that there are cards for every situation, including "Sorry to hear your pet died" and "Congratulations on your new apartment," to name a few. So, depending on what you want to communicate at any given time, you can choose a card that best expresses those thoughts and feelings.

Believe it or not, prayer is a lot like greeting cards. In the Catholic tradition, there are five forms of prayer, or five primary reasons why people turn to God in prayer. They are actually very similar to some of the topics you find in greeting cards. And like the sections in a greeting card store, these forms serve to identify just about everything you'd ever want to communicate in prayer to God. The five primary reasons for praying are (1) to bless and adore God, (2) to petition God for forgiveness or some other personal need, (3) to intercede or to ask God for something on the behalf of others, (4) to thank God, and (5) to praise God.

As you can see, we hold our focus on God whenever we pray in blessing, praise, or thanksgiving. What we want to communicate is how great we think God is and how grateful we are for all the things God continually does for us. Those are pretty good reasons for praying. That's why so many of the Church's official prayers tend to express praise and gratitude to God. In prayers of petition and intercession, we seek to tell God about the needs we have and to ask God for help, help for others and help for ourselves. Where did the Church learn to group its prayers into these topics? From Jesus!

Catechism Key

The Holy Spirit who teaches the Church and recalls to her all that Jesus said also instructs her in the life of prayer, inspiring new expressions of the same basic forms of prayer: blessing, petition, intercession, thanksgiving, and praise. (2644)

Send the very best

You are browsing through a Christian greeting card store. There are five categories of cards: Blessing, Praise, Thanksgiving, Petition, and Intercession. For each of the five greeting cards below, write a short verse addressed to God that fits each category.

Blessing

Praise

Thanksgiving

Petition

Intercession

Now you know there's nothing to composing a prayer. It's as simple as writing a personal message in a greeting card. All you have to do is speak from your heart!

Pray in the Spirit at all times in every prayer and supplication. To that end keep alert and always persevere in supplication for all the saints.

—Ephesians 6:18

When you offer prayers of intercession for other people, what do you often pray for?

_____

_____

_____

The Lord's Prayer

[Jesus] was praying in a certain place, and after he had finished, one of his disciples said to him, "Lord, teach us to pray, as John taught his disciples." He said to them, "When you pray, say:

> *Father, hallowed be your name.*
> *Your kingdom come.*
> *Give us each day our daily bread.*
> *And forgive us our sins,*
> *   for we ourselves forgive everyone*
> *   indebted to us.*
> *And do not bring us to the time of*
> *   trial."*

—Luke 11:1–4

When Jesus' disciples asked him to teach them to pray, he gave them what we now call the Lord's Prayer. As you might expect, the Lord's Prayer has become one of the Church's most used prayers. It has an official place in the Eucharist, for example, and in the celebration of other sacraments. It's been called the *Little Gospel* because it gives us an excellent summary of core truths Jesus reveals to us throughout the New Testament. You may be familiar with the Lord's Prayer, but let's examine each of its parts so we can better see what Jesus is teaching us about how to pray to God the Father.

The Church traditionally divides the prayer into these segments:

I. The Address

• Our Father, who art in heaven

II. The Seven Petitions

1. Hallowed be your name

2. Your kingdom come

3. Your will be done on earth as it is in heaven

4. Give us this day our daily bread

5. And forgive us our trespasses as we forgive those who trespass against us

6. And lead us not into temptation

7. But deliver us from evil

A Prayer Tradition ✠

After his twenty-ninth birthday, Siddhartha Gautama (563–486 B.C.E.) went in search of peace and salvation. For seven years he meditated on the causes for evil, the means to happiness and peace, and the meaning of life. Finally, Gautama discovered The Four Noble or Sacred Truths of the way to enlightenment. Gautama received the name the Buddha meaning "The Enlightened One." This was the beginning of Buddhism.

The address

The Lord's Prayer starts out, as all prayer should, by raising our hearts and minds to God. We begin by addressing God. But it is important to note how Jesus tells us we should look to and address God—as "our Father." We can call God *Father* because the Son of God revealed him to us and it is through the Spirit that we come to know God. Above all else, Jesus wants us to understand that we have nothing to fear when we turn to God in prayer. In fact, everyone should approach God with love, trust, and confidence, much like a small child approaches and calls out to a loving, caring parent.

Also, it is no accident that Jesus teaches us to pray "Our Father" rather than "My Father." Even though prayer always has a very personal dimension to it, we are members of God's family and have a responsibility to our brothers and sisters; therefore we should pray to God on the behalf of all people.

In the second half of the address—"who art in heaven"—Jesus teaches another important truth. *Heaven* used here doesn't mean a place. Rather it calls our attention to the divine nature of the One we dare to call our Father. Though Jesus always urges us to think of and approach God as our Father, he also wants us to remember that this loving, gentle, caring Father remains God—the awesome, mysterious, all-powerful Creator and Lord of all that is. So when you approach God in prayer, your childlike sense of intimacy should always include a deep sense of reverence and respect, too.

Focus on God

Each of the seven statements that follow the opening address takes the form of a request or a *petition*. In this way, Jesus is making it clear to us that all good prayer starts by accepting our limitations and realizing our dependence on God. Remember, it is the basic awareness of our limitations that moves us to seek God in the first place.

Notice that the first three petitions aren't requests for personal favors; rather they focus on God and what we should want for God. In the first petition, for example—"hallowed be

your name"—Jesus teaches us we should desire above all else that God be honored and respected for who God is: the all-holy God and the source of all holiness. *Hallowed* means "holy." In asking that God's name be made holy, we are saying we want God's holiness to be recognized and respected. We are expressing the desire that God be honored and loved—at all times, everywhere, and by everyone. So this first petition really is a perfect and profound prayer of adoration and praise.

Next Jesus directs us to pray "Your kingdom come." This kingdom or reign of God will become fully present at the end of time. Then the human family will fully experience the perfect "righteousness and peace and joy in the Holy Spirit" (Romans 14:17), which Jesus has won for us and God has intended for us since the beginning of time. Jesus is

teaching us to keep our focus on God's ultimate goal for us. God's reign should be the second most important thing you seek in prayers of petition—after asking for God's forgiveness.

The third petition, "Your will be done on earth as it is in heaven" is similar to the second petition, but now the focus is on our need to know and carry out what God wants us to do here on earth so that the kingdom may finally come. After seeking God's honor and God's plan for creation, Jesus wants us to pray that we—and all people—carry out God's will in our day-to-day life and decisions. Doing God's will is actually the best way to praise God and also to hasten the coming of God's kingdom.

The last four petitions of the Lord's Prayer all use the word "us" as opposed to "me." Why do you think Jesus asked that we pray the Lord's Prayer this way?

_____

_____

_____

_____

Our daily bread

In the next petition of the Lord's Prayer, Jesus teaches us to say "Give us this day our daily bread." But why do we say "give us" instead of "give me"? Think back to the reason why we say "our Father" rather than "my Father." God is the Creator of all people, and we are to pray to God on the behalf of everyone, in suffering and in happiness. We are called to be aware of the needs of others and to share God's gifts with everyone. After all, this kind of sharing and concern for others is what the Eucharist is all about. But in order to accomplish what Jesus has directed, we must live in union and harmony with all people. God excludes no one from his gifts.

Note in this petition how Jesus says to ask for the bread "daily." Why daily? Why not a month's supply at a time or all we need for the rest of our lives? Suppose God gave you a year's supply of something all at once. There's a good chance you would forget about God (from whom all your gifts come) because you no longer needed to turn to God on a regular basis. For this reason, Jesus wanted to stress how important it is to remember every day our dependence on God.

The bread we ask of God when we pray "Give us this day our daily bread" refers first of all to our basic material needs, such as food, clothing, and shelter. It also refers to our spiritual needs, which are satisfied when we celebrate the Eucharist together. Jesus reminds us that all these things are ultimately gifts that come from our loving Creator. As God's beloved children, we have the right to turn to God confidently and to express our needs. By teaching us to ask for bread, Jesus also reminds us to focus on the basics, the things we really need. After all, nothing is more basic than bread. And God promises to provide us with the basic things we need.

Just the basics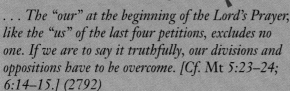

List the ten top things you feel make up your daily bread as it means in the Lord's Prayer.

1.

2.

3.

4.

5.

6.

7.

8.

9.

10.

Catechism Key

. . . The "our" at the beginning of the Lord's Prayer, like the "us" of the last four petitions, excludes no one. If we are to say it truthfully, our divisions and oppositions have to be overcome. [Cf. Mt 5:23–24; 6:14–15.] (2792)

Forgive one another

Jesus is a realist. He knows all too well that sin and selfishness have been a part of human life since the Fall of Adam and Eve when original sin entered the world. At times, we may all stray and become entrapped in selfishness and in our indifference to God and to others. So the next petition in the Lord's Prayer is clear enough. Jesus encourages us to admit our sinfulness and to confidently approach our loving Father, seeking forgiveness. We ask God the Father to "Forgive us our trespasses" (sins, selfishness). But there is a catch, isn't there? We can ask forgiveness only "in the way that we forgive those who trespass against us."

For if you forgive others their trespasses, your heavenly Father will also forgive you; but if you do not forgive others, neither will your Father forgive your trespasses.

—*Matthew 6:14–15*

Carefully think about the events of the past two weeks. Is there anyone you need to forgive for something done during this time? Did anything happen that you need to be forgiven for? Explain what you will do to make things right.

_____
_____
_____
_____
_____

Scripture Sketch

Take a minute and read the parable of the merciless official in Matthew 18:21–35. How does this parable help explain the meaning behind the fifth petition of the Lord's Prayer: "Forgive us our trespasses as we forgive those who trespass against us"?

_____
_____
_____
_____
_____

Protect us from evil

After praying for the physical and spiritual gifts we need to live and grow, Jesus teaches us to turn to God for protection from those things that can harm us spiritually and physically. It's obvious God doesn't go around tempting us to do evil. So by praying "Lead us not into temptation," we are in fact asking God to guide us **away from** the things and situations that can trip us up. We ask God to show us the right way and to give us the courage to reject and turn away from false values, the quick fix, the easy (and sinful) way out.

In an average day, many bad things may happen. Some we have no control over, such as hurricanes and tornadoes, floods and droughts, sickness and disease. Some bad things have a direct human involvement, such as war, violence, and crime. Jesus teaches us to turn to our loving Creator and confidently ask for protection from all such evils. The ultimate evil, of course, is Satan, or the Evil One. Satan's goal is to turn us away from God and goodness. When we pray "but deliver us from evil," we ask God to turn us away from all evil, both physical and spiritual.

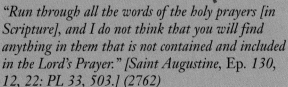

Catechism Key

"Run through all the words of the holy prayers [in Scripture], and I do not think that you will find anything in them that is not contained and included in the Lord's Prayer." [Saint Augustine, Ep. 130, 12, 22: PL 33, 503.] (2762)

Guidelines for prayer

After praying the Lord's Prayer for many years, you may never have truly understood its meaning. It's easy to recite something from memory without ever listening to what is really being said. Although we've just analyzed it in a single chapter, it may take some time to truly comprehend all that the prayer says. But the Lord's Prayer is the perfect prayer and can tell us everything we need to know about praying. The following are the basics of what the Lord's Prayer teaches about prayer. Following these guidelines, you pray in the way Jesus taught his disciples.

1. When you pray, always remember that you are turning to your loving Father. So pray in the spirit of a little child—with total confidence and trust.

2. Pray with humility. Remember that you need God always. Rely on God's grace.

3. Keep your priorities and values straight; God's honor, God's kingdom, and God's forgiveness should be at the top of the list of things you pray for.

4. God expects you to ask for what you need to live and grow, both physically and spiritually. God is eager to give those things, provided that you share the gifts God gives. So ask God with confidence every day for these gifts.

5. Sometimes your prayer will serve as an apology, asking your loving God for forgiveness. Just remember that you can't really expect God to forgive you if you aren't willing to forgive those who have hurt you. Being unwilling to forgive others is actually a sign that you aren't really sorry for your own sins. Being willing to forgive others is a way of accepting God's forgiveness.

6. Finally, your prayer should focus on asking God for guidance and protection from all forms of harm or evil, both physical and spiritual. The worst evil of all is to be tricked by Satan into rejecting God and God's love for you.

Scripture Sketch

Read the story of the Pharisee and the tax collector who go to the temple to pray (Luke 18:9–14). What does this story teach you about prayer?

_____
_____
_____
_____
_____

God is interested in you!

In one sense, all you'd ever have to do to have a good prayer life is to pray the Lord's Prayer regularly and thoughtfully. But it is also good to use your own words to express your praise and thanks. We should talk to God about our own personal needs, for specific kinds of help, to seek forgiveness for specific sins and misdeeds. Some people get trapped into thinking that their personal prayer must be like the formal prayers they hear, with words such as "thee," "thou," and "beseech." But that isn't how you talk with a good friend, is it?

But what should you say? Well, when talking with a good friend, you can discuss a wide variety of topics. Take a look at the opening activity for this chapter on page twelve. The things you listed in that activity are probably some of the same topics you would discuss with a friend—school, the recent soccer game, your family, your favorite musician. Sometimes you may wish to share a problem or ask for advice. At times, you may need to apologize for something you did or said. Or you may wish to thank your friend for his or her help.

When you turn to God in prayer, why not talk about and share these same things? After all, personal prayer means communicating personal things—your thoughts, needs, fears, and concerns, your successes and failures, your interests and adventures. Everything you listed in the opening activity for the chapter would be worthwhile to talk to God about in prayer.

So when you want to raise your mind and heart to God, remember that what you should bring to your prayer is **your** mind and heart— what is happening in your life and what is important to you. That's what God wants you to share. If in the process you follow Jesus' guidelines for praying, you'll do just fine. You'll be praying the way Jesus taught all his disciples to pray to his loving Father.

Pause to Pray

Dear Lord,
Help us remember your kindness and generosity as we bless you
  for all our gifts.
Give us the courage to ask forgiveness for our sins and to
  change our ways.
Help us always to pray for and care for all people.
Thank you for your bountiful gifts and for your loving guidance.
We praise your glory forever and ever.
Amen.

Reflection

Reader 1: "Our Father, who art in heaven . . ."

Reader 2: Yes.

Reader 1: Don't interrupt me. I'm praying.

Reader 2: But you called me.

Reader 1: Called you? I didn't call you. I'm praying. "Our Father, who art in heaven . . ."

Reader 2: There, you did it again.

Reader 1: Did what?

Reader 2: Called me. You said, "Our Father, who art in heaven." Here I am. What's on your mind?

Reader 1: But I didn't mean anything by it. I was, you know, just saying my prayers for the day. I always say the Lord's Prayer. It makes me feel good; kind of like getting a duty done.

Reader 2: All right, go on.

Reader 1: "Hallowed be your name."

Reader 2: Hold it. What did you mean by that?

Reader 1: By what?

Reader 2: By "Hallowed by your name."

Reader 1: It means . . . it means . . . good grief, I don't know what it means. How should I know? It's just part of the prayer. By the way, what does it mean?

Reader 2: It means honored, holy, wonderful.

Reader 1: Hey, that makes sense. I never thought what "hallowed" meant before. "Your kingdom come; your will be done on earth as it is in heaven."

Reader 2: Do you really mean that?

Reader 1: Sure, why not?

Reader 2: What are you doing about it?

Reader 1: Doing? Nothing, I guess. I just think it would be kind of neat if you got control of everything down here like you have up there.

Reader 2: Have I got control of you?

Reader 1: Well, I go to church.

Reader 2: That isn't what I asked you. What about that habit of lust you have? And your bad temper? You've really got a problem there, the way you spend your money . . . all on yourself. And what about the kind of books you read?

24

Reader 1: Stop picking on me! I'm just as good as some of the rest of those phonies at church.

Reader 2: Excuse me. I thought you were praying for my will to be done. If that is to happen, it will have to start with the ones who are praying for it. Like you, for example.

Reader 1: Oh, all right. I guess I do have some hang-ups. Now that you mention it, I probably could name some others.

Reader 2: So could I.

Reader 1: I haven't thought about it very much until now. But I really would like to cut out some of those things. I would like to, you know, be really free.

Reader 2: Good. Now we're getting somewhere. We'll work together, you and I. Some victories can truly be won. I'm proud of you.

Reader 1: Look, Lord, I need to finish up here. This is taking a lot longer than it usually does. "Give us this day our daily bread."

Reader 2: You need to cut out the bread. You're overweight as it is.

Reader 1: Hey, wait a minute! What is this, "Criticize Me Day"? Here I was doing my religious duty, and all of a sudden you break in and remind me of all my hang-ups.

Reader 2: Praying is a dangerous thing. You could wind up changed, you know. That's what I'm trying to get across to you. You called me, and here I am. It's too late to stop now. Keep praying; I'm interested in the next part of your prayer . . . Well, go on.

Reader 1: I'm scared to.

Reader 2: Scared? Of what?

Reader 1: I know what you'll say.

Reader 2: Try me and see.

Reader 1: "And forgive us our trespasses as we forgive those who trespass against us."

Reader 2: What about Erin?

Reader 1: See? I knew it! I knew you would bring her up. Why, Lord, she told lies about me, cheated me out of some money. She never paid back that debt she owes me. I've sworn to get even with her.

Reader 2: But what about your prayer?

Reader 1: I didn't mean it.

Reader 2: Well, at least you're honest. But it's not much fun carrying that load of bitterness around inside, is it?

Reader 1: No, but I'll feel better as soon as I get even. Boy, have I got some plans for old Erin. She'll wish she never did me any harm.

Reader 2: You won't feel any better. You'll feel worse. Revenge isn't sweet. Think of how unhappy you already are. But I can change all that.

Reader 1: You can? How?

Reader 2: Forgive Erin as I have forgiven you. Then the hate and sin will be Erin's problems, not yours. You may lose the money, but you will have settled your heart.

Reader 1: But Lord, I can't forgive Erin.

Reader 2: Then I can't forgive you.

Reader 1: Oh, you're right. You always are. And more than I want revenge on Erin, I want to be right with you . . . (sigh). All right. All right. I forgive her. Help her to find the right road in life. She's bound to be awfully miserable now that I think about it. Anybody who goes around doing the things that she does to others has to be out of it. Some way, somehow, show her the right way. And, Lord, help me to forget it too.

Reader 2: There now! Wonderful! How do you feel?

25

Reader 1: Hmmmm, well, not bad. Not bad at all. In fact, I feel pretty great! You know, I don't think I'll have to go to bed uptight tonight for the first time since I can remember. Maybe I won't be so tired from now on because I'm not getting enough rest.

Reader 2: You're not through with your prayer.

Reader 1: Oh, all right. "And lead us not into temptation, but deliver us from evil."

Reader 2: Good! Good! I'll do that. Just don't put yourself in a place where you can be tempted.

Reader 1: What do you mean by that?

Reader 2: Quit hanging around with that group that's always getting into trouble. Change some of your friendships. Some of your so-called friends are beginning to get to you. They'll have you completely involved in wrong things before long. Don't be fooled. They advertise they're having fun, but for you it would be ruin. Don't use me for an escape hatch.

Reader 1: I don't understand.

Reader 2: Sure you do. You've done it lots of times. You get in bad situations, get into trouble and then come running to me. "Lord, help me out of this mess, and I promise I'll never do it again." You remember some of those bargains you tried to make with me?

Reader 1: Yes, and I'm ashamed, Lord. I really am.

Reader 2: Which bargain are you remembering?

Reader 1: Well, the time I almost got caught cheating on a test. I remember telling you: "Oh Lord, don't let her tell the teacher. If she doesn't, I promise I'll be in church every Sunday and do anything you want me to do."

Reader 2: She didn't tell, but you didn't keep your promise, did you?

Reader 1: I'm sorry, Lord. I really am. Up until now I thought that if I just prayed the Lord's Prayer every day, I could do what I like. I didn't expect anything to happen like this . . . that you really listen.

Reader 2: Go ahead and finish your prayer.

Reader 1: "For the kingdom, the power, and the glory are yours, now and forever. Amen."

Reader 2: Do you know what would bring me glory? What would really make me happy?

Reader 1: No. But I'd like to know. I want to please you. I can see what a mess I've made of my life. And I can see how neat it would be to really be one of your followers.

Reader 2: You just answered the question.

Reader 1: I did?

Reader 2: Yes. The thing that would bring me glory is to have people like you truly love me. And I see that happening between us. Now that some of these old sins are exposed and out of the way, well, there's no telling what we can do together.

Reader 1: Lord, let's see what we can make of me. Okay?

Reader 2: Yes. Let's see.

Excerpt adapted from *If God Talked Out Loud*, by Clyde Lee Herring. (Nashville, TN: Broadman Press, 1977).

Homework

Open your Bible to the Book of Psalms. Find five psalms that are examples of each of the five forms of prayer. Write in the space provided the number of the psalm and a brief description of what it says about prayer.

Psalm of Blessing: _____

Psalm of Praise: _____

Psalm of Thanksgiving: _____

Psalm of Petition: _____

Psalm of Intercession: _____

Extra! Extra!

In your own words and with your own thoughts and feelings, please answer the title of this chapter: What should I say? Your answer should be a paragraph of fifty words or more. Write your answer on page 99 in the appendix.

What's the Answer?

Three Wishes

A wise person once said, "Be careful what you ask for. You may just get it." You may remember a popular television commercial that illustrates this point. A genie appears before a man and offers him three wishes. For his first wish, he asks for great wealth. Poof! He is surrounded by piles of money, gold, silver, and jewels. Second, the man wishes for beautiful girlfriends. Poof! He is surrounded by many beautiful women. Finally, the man asks for long life. Poof! He is turned into the Energizer Bunny.

If God were to offer to grant you three wishes today, what would you wish for? Think carefully before you write down your answers.

- Wish One: _____
- Wish Two: _____
- Wish Three: _____

"Ask, and you will receive"

As we saw in the last chapter, prayers of petition (where we seek God's help) aren't necessarily the most important form of prayer. But if we're honest, we probably say prayers of petition more often than any other form of prayer. That's perfectly okay; we have Jesus' word for it. In fact, Jesus spent a lot of time teaching his followers how to ask for his Father's help. Here are just a few "tips" Jesus gave us:

- Praying with others can be especially effective (Matthew 18:19–20).
- Pray with confidence; God knows what you need (Luke 12:27–31).
- The more faith you have, the more effective your prayer (Luke 17:5–6).
- If at first you don't succeed, try again and again (Luke 18:1–7).
- Whatever you need, ask for it in Jesus' name (John 14:13).

Jesus stressed over and over that our loving God always hears **and** answers sincere prayers. For example, he once said, "Ask, and you will receive. Search, and you will find. Knock, and the door will be opened for you" (Matthew 7:7–8). In fact, there are many places in the Gospels where we find Jesus himself saying a prayer of petition and asking for God the Father's help in carrying out his mission. So when you pray, don't be afraid to ask for what you need.

Scripture Sketch

Read each of these Scripture passages in your Bible: Matthew 18:19–20, Luke 12:27–31, Luke 17:5–6, Luke 18:1–7, John 14:13. Then give an example from your own life for each of the passages.

Matthew 18:19–20 _____

Luke 12:27–31 _____

Luke 17:5–6 _____

Luke 18:1–7 _____

John 14:13 _____

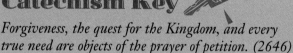

And do not keep striving for what you are to eat and what you are to drink, and do not keep worrying. For it is the nations of the world that strive after all these things, and your Father knows that you need them. Instead, strive for his kingdom, and these things will be given to you as well.

—*Luke 12:29–31*

What do you spend most of your time praying for?

_____

_____

_____

_____

Take some time to think about your priorities. Are they what God really wants for you?

_____

_____

_____

_____

Catechism Key

Forgiveness, the quest for the Kingdom, and every true need are objects of the prayer of petition. (2646)

God knows what we need

You may have been told that "God answers all your prayers; it's just that sometimes the answer is no." That's not completely true. It's more accurate to say that God answers all your prayers but only gives you what you really need, not what you think you need. Sometimes what people think is important may not be what is best for them. It's similar to the way parents deal with little children. A two-year-old may want to play with shiny scissors, but her dad gives her a soft toy instead. So God, like the good parent, really wants us to be happy. It's just that sometimes what we think will make us happy is not the same as what God knows we need.

Here's an example. It's the end of the school year, and you have a very important test on Friday. If you don't pass the test, you must go to summer school. But your friend asks you to go to the movies on Thursday night. You spend all evening with your friend and never get around to studying for the test. You pray to God to help you pass the test. But God doesn't come through with

the right answers; and you fail the test. Has God let you down or broken the promise to answer all your prayers? Not really. God gives you a "wake-up call" instead. You see, God has probably already given you all the natural talents you need to pass the test. So when you fail the test, God is signaling you to use your natural talents, which God knows you really need to earn good grades.

A Prayer Tradition

Hindus believe that there are four ways to achieve union with Ultimate Reality—through knowledge (Jnana Yoga), through love (Bhakti Yoga), through work (Karma Yoga), and through psychological experience (Raja Yoga). These four kinds of yoga give specific directions to achieve spiritual goals.

29

From lemons to lemonade

When we're in a bad situation, often we try to find something positive in the experience. God answers prayers in this way, too. For example, instead of solving your immediate problem, God sometimes helps you discover new solutions and new possibilities in what seems like a bad situation. To put it another way, God doesn't take away the lemon you've been given but shows you how to make lemonade with it.

For example, a factory employee learns that his company is going to lay off 100 employees. He desperately prays to God that he won't be one of those laid off, but he is. After some struggle and hard times, he finally finds a new job. He enjoys the work and the people and is much happier than he was at his old job. He even earns more money at his new job. Although being out of work wasn't a pleasant experience, he realizes that it was a blessing when God led him to the new, better job rather than giving him what he thought he wanted.

Describe a bad situation you experienced that resulted in something positive. What lemon did you turn into lemonade?

_____
_____
_____
_____

God's angels

In the Greek language the word *angel* means "messenger." Many people tend to think of angels as holy and powerful spirits God sends from heaven to help someone or to deliver a message. Sometimes the Gospel stories describe angels in this way. But not all messengers from God are invisible spirits who come from heaven. Sometimes God's messengers come from next door or from the desk behind you in class.

You see, many times the "angels" God uses to answer our prayers are real people just like you. And most of the time these angels aren't even aware they are doing God's work. For example, a woman's car breaks down on a lonely stretch of highway at night. She is frightened and utters a quick prayer to God for help. A few minutes later, a highway patrol car pulls over, and the officer offers his help. The officer is an "angel" to the woman, even though he is just doing his job.

God often answers prayers by guiding ordinary people doing ordinary things to come to another person's rescue and provide for their needs. At times, even you may be one of God's angels, the one God sends to answer another person's prayers!

Describe a time when one of God's angels helped you.

_____

_____

_____

_____

Describe a time when you served as one of God's angels for another person.

_____

_____

_____

_____

Patience is a virtue

Today everyone is in a hurry. We expect instant solutions to every problem. If our needs are not satisfied immediately, we become impatient and frustrated. However, God isn't obligated to follow our clock or calendar. Though God does answer all our prayers, sometimes we need to keep praying, patiently waiting for an answer.

The Church throughout the world prayed every day at Mass for over fifty years that the people of the Soviet Union would be free from communism. A few years ago, as you know, God finally answered all those prayers—in God's time!

Interestingly, the pope at the time was from Poland. John Paul II was a very influential person in the changing attitudes that led to the end of communism. In God's time!

Saint Monica, the mother of Saint Augustine, prayed every day for more than twenty years for the conversion of her son to Christianity. After all those years, her son not only was baptized as a Christian but became the bishop of Hippo, as well as one of the greatest saints and theologians in the Church's history.

Why does God sometimes take so long to answer our prayers? There's no sure answer; but this much we know: God always answers our prayers at the **best time**—when we are truly ready and when it will do the most good.

On a scale of 1 to 5, with 1 being the highest, how would you rate your level of patience? _____
In what ways can you work to improve your level of patience?

_____

_____

_____

A Prayer Tradition

Faithful followers of Judaism recite the Shema *at morning and evening services, as well as in private. The Shema summarizes Judaism's strong faith in and love of God. You can read the Shema in Deuteronomy 6:4–9.*

God's will be done

Perhaps the most important thing you need to know about how God answers your prayers is taught in this passage from the Gospel of Mark:

And going a little farther, [Jesus] threw himself on the ground and prayed that, if it were possible, the hour might pass from him. He said, "Abba, Father, for you all things are possible; remove this cup from me; yet, not what I want, but what you want."

—Mark 14:35–36

Some background on this passage may help to understand why Jesus said what he did. The setting is Gethsemane. Jesus is about to be arrested, tortured, and crucified. He really doesn't like the idea, to say the least, and asks God the Father to rescue him. He has no doubt that his Father has the power to save him; so faith and trust aren't an issue. But Jesus also understands that God the Father wants what is best, not just for Jesus, but for everyone. If his Father sees Jesus' crucifixion as necessary and good, Jesus will accept the decision even if he doesn't fully understand it. So after Jesus tells his Father what he would like, he adds, "Yet, not what I want, but what you want."

The point is never to be afraid to ask for what you want and what you think you need. But pray most of all that *God's will be done,* since what God wants is ultimately best for you and for everyone else—even if at the time you don't understand how it is best for anyone. In fact, this is often how God answers our prayers—not by doing what we ask, but by helping us discover and then fully accept God's plan, just as Jesus did. Learning to recognize, accept, and then follow God's will is ultimately the best way God answers our prayers.

There will be times when, after praying long and hard for something you really want, you come to realize that you don't need it. You understand that God actually answered your prayer by helping you see that what you thought you wanted wasn't really the best thing for you. Often the real answer to your prayers is that you are able to see things differently, the way God sees things.

It's a miracle!

People usually think of a miracle as a supernatural event; God intervenes in life by setting aside the laws of nature to help someone or to bring about some good. That's one way to think of miracles. God certainly has the power to act that way. But there is another way to understand miracles. A miracle does not depend so much on **how** God intervenes to help, but it depends on recognizing **that** God intervenes to help.

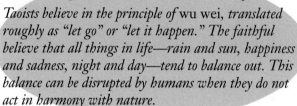

A Prayer Tradition

Taoists believe in the principle of wu wei, *translated roughly as "let go" or "let it happen." The faithful believe that all things in life—rain and sun, happiness and sadness, night and day—tend to balance out. This balance can be disrupted by humans when they do not act in harmony with nature.*

Many of the miracles recorded in the Hebrew Scriptures, for example, weren't necessarily supernatural events where God set aside the laws of nature. They were natural events. But through the eyes of faith, the Hebrews came to recognize God's loving care and help at work in these events. Most of the ten plagues that befell the Egyptians (Exodus 7–10) were actually natural events, such as flooding, hail, and dust storms. It's just that the Hebrews understood that God was using these natural events as a means to free them from their slavery.

So not all things called miracles are supernatural events. In fact, most miracles can seem quite natural at first glance. But with the eyes of faith, we recognize God's loving care and help at work in these natural events. For example, it is true that Jesus occasionally gave sight to a physically blind person, using what we can consider supernatural powers. But what about all the times Jesus gave "sight" to a person blinded by fear or hatred or ignorance—simply by talking with and being kind to that person. In a sense, it was just as much a miracle to cure the spiritual blindness of Zacchaeus as it was to cure the physical blindness of Bartimaeus, a beggar near Jericho.

It's not that God can't or does not intervene and answer prayers in what can be described as supernatural ways. (Even then, Pope John Paul II tells us that miracles do not have to be thought of as violating laws of nature.) Some call these acts "wonders" or "marvels." But it seems that most often God uses ordinary means and the existing laws of nature to answer our prayers and to bring about "miraculous" results. There are "miracles" happening all the time if you look at life with the eyes of faith.

In fact, Jesus promised that you, as one of his followers, have the power to work wonders, too. Have you ever helped a friend overcome some crippling fear or sadness? If you did, you gave a "lame" person new legs. Have you ever helped two people put aside their anger and become friends again? If you did, you restored a friendship to life, which is no small "miracle." Have you helped a friend see that experimenting with some drug is dangerous rather than cool? If you did, you gave sight to a "blind" person.

So when you pray, you can expect miracles. Just remember it often takes the eyes of faith to recognize God's "miraculous" activities in your life.

Scripture Sketch

Read in Luke 19:1–10 the story of the spiritual healing of Zacchaeus, a tax collector. Write a short story, fact or fiction, of someone who has undergone a similar healing.

_____

_____

_____

_____

_____

_____

_____

_____

_____

_____

_____

_____

Describe a time when you asked God for help and feel you didn't receive an answer. Now knowing the many ways God answers prayers, explain how God answered your prayer.

_____

_____

_____

Prayer is (or is not) . . .

Listed below are a few mistakes people make when praying prayers of petition. You may want to check to see if you have made any of these mistakes.

1. **Thinking prayer is magic.** In this sense, magic is not an illusion or trick. Magic in religious language is the mistaken idea that we can "force" God to grant our wishes if we say the right words or perform certain rituals. Many ancient peoples practiced this kind of "magic" religion. A common form of magic we see today is the belief in superstition. Chain letters that circulate through schools and communities are an example of superstition. The letters usually predict that something terrible will happen if the directions stated in the letter are not followed. Just remember the real purpose of prayers of petition is to align our will with God's will, not the reverse. Thinking we can control God through some special prayer formula or ritual is ridiculous.

2. **Praying for things we really don't need.** *The Catechism of the Catholic Church* instructs us to pray for every true need. Winning the championship game, getting the highest grade in class, or winning the lottery are good things, but none of them are true necessities. Life will go on if your team loses the game, if you get a passing grade, or if you don't win the lottery. So don't be surprised if nothing happens if you aren't praying for things you truly need.

3. **Praying for evil.** Obviously God will not respond to a prayer of petition for something that is evil. God will not help anyone get revenge on or bring harm to another person.

4. **Praying for things when we are unwilling to do our part ourselves.** There's a Russian proverb that says, "If you get caught in a storm on the lake, pray to God, but keep rowing toward shore." This idea was discussed earlier in the chapter. Don't bother asking for God's help to pass a test if you aren't willing to do your part by studying for it.

5. **Not being sincere.** Some people never bother to pray except when they need something. The rest of the time they go about their life without ever giving any thought to God. Then in an emergency they turn to God with a quick cry for help and get upset when God doesn't immediately answer their prayers. Remember, God answers only **sincere** prayers. These "only in case of emergency" prayers usually aren't sincere forms of prayer.

6. **Giving up too soon.** Jesus stressed that we need to be patient and persistent when we ask for God's help. Some people aren't willing to commit to the "long haul" when they start praying. They ask for help once or twice (often without doing their part); and if nothing happens, they give up and often complain that God doesn't care.

Learning from our mistakes

Below is the list of common mistakes people often make when praying a prayer of petition. Rank them (1, 2, 3, . . .) in terms of the mistakes you think people your age are most likely to make (1) to the mistakes people are least likely to make (6).

_____ Thinking prayer is magic.

_____ Praying for something you don't really need.

_____ Praying for something that is evil.

_____ Praying for something when you are unwilling to do your part yourself.

_____ Not being sincere.

_____ Giving up too soon.

Pause to Pray

To you, O LORD, I lift up my soul.
O my God, in you I trust;
  do not let me be put to shame;
  do not let my enemies exult over me.
Do not let those who wait for you be put to shame;
  let them be ashamed who are wantonly treacherous.
Make me to know your ways, O LORD;
  teach me your paths.
Lead me in your truth, and teach me,
  for you are the God of my salvation;
  for you I wait all day long.
Be mindful of your mercy, O LORD, and of your steadfast love,
  for they have been from of old.
Do not remember the sins of my youth or my transgressions;
  according to your steadfast love remember me,
  for your goodness' sake, O LORD!
                    —Psalm 25:1–7

Reader 1: God, I hate this new town. Why didn't you answer my prayers and let my family stay at our old home? Why didn't you help me?

Reader 2: Keesha, you don't think I listen to you?

Reader 1: God? Well, uh, you didn't answer my prayers for help. I didn't want to move.

Reader 2: I know. But what about your family? Your parents moved because your dad got a new job after being out of work for nine months. I think moving was best for your whole family.

Reader 1: I know, and I'm happy for Dad and Mom. But I'm so lonely. I miss everyone from home, especially Amy. We've been friends since kindergarten.

Reader 2: You don't think you'll make new friends?

Reader 1: But it's so hard. Why won't you help me?

Reader 2: Well, first you have to help yourself. You may actually have to leave your bedroom and your house to meet new people.

Reader 1: Thanks a lot.

Reader 2: Relax and be patient. You'll make new friends as well as keep your old friends. You've only been here two days. Talk to your dad. He knows how to be patient.

Reader 1: Huh?

Reader 2: Well, he prayed for months and months for a job. He could have given up; but he never did. And sure enough, eventually he was offered a better job than the one he had before.

Reader 1: I never thought of that.

Reader 3: Keesha, Maddie from next door is here to see you.

Reader 1: Maddie? I think I met her on the day we moved.

Reader 2: I know.

Reader 1: You know?

Reader 2: I asked Maddie to help you. She's one of my special angels.

Reader 1: An angel from heaven?

Reader 2: No, an angel from next door.

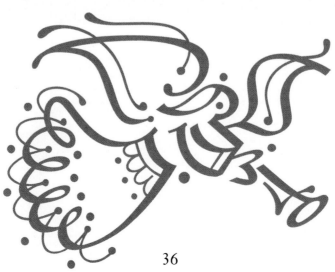

36

Homework

In Luke's Gospel, there are three principal parables on prayer. Through these parables, Jesus gives us instructions for our prayer life. Write in your own words a "rule for prayer" based on each instruction.

- Luke 6:27–31

Rule: _____

- Luke 11:5–13

Rule: _____

- Luke 22:39–46

Rule: _____

Extra! Extra!

In your own words and with your own thoughts and feelings, please answer the title of this chapter: What's the answer? Your answer should be a paragraph of fifty words or more. Write your answer on page 99 in the appendix.

How Should I Pray?

Can we talk? Part I

There are many different ways people express their thoughts and feelings to others. While most of us enjoy communicating, we don't all enjoy communicating in the same way. Below is a list of ways to communicate with other people. Select from the list your favorite form of communication, and put a ✓ in front of the item. Choose your least favorite way of communicating by putting an ✗ in front of the item. Be prepared to share your choices with your group.

- ❏ Talk one-on-one
- ❏ Write a letter
- ❏ Send an e-mail message
- ❏ Talk on the telephone
- ❏ Chat on the Internet
- ❏ Send a greeting card
- ❏ Talk in front of a large group
- ❏ Use sign language
- ❏ Other: _____

So many choices

People of all religions all over the world pray or communicate with God. But how do these people pray? Is there one standard way of praying for each religion? Of course not. There are many different ways or styles of prayer.

To understand the many different ways or styles of prayer, take a look at how you communicate with the people around you. How we communicate depends on whom we are communicating with and what we want to say. If your best friend lives in Europe, you may choose to write him a letter or send a greeting card. On special occasions, you may choose to call him on the telephone. But if your best friend lives next door, then you could easily visit with him in person. At times we communicate our thoughts together with others, such as cheering at a basketball game or clapping at a concert. Or we communicate physically with a hug, a handshake, or a pat on the back. And sometimes we communicate the loudest when we say nothing, such as holding a friend's hand as she lies in a hospital bed.

So we spend a great portion of our lives communicating with others in many different ways. Well, the Church also has many ways to communicate with God, many different forms of prayer. Just like the forms of communication, you will probably find some forms of prayer more appealing to you than others. Some forms will be better suited for one situation, and others will work best in a different situation. But as you examine the different ways to pray, just remember that all of them are good and all can lead to the same result—communion with God.

Can we talk? Part II

There are many different ways to pray and many different places to pray. From the list below, select your favorite way to pray by putting a ✓ in front of the item. Select your least favorite way to pray by putting an ✗ in front of the item. Be prepared to share your choices with your group.

❑ At Mass or other formal celebrations

❑ By reading or reciting formal prayers such as the Lord's Prayer

❑ By talking to God using my own words

❑ By reading passages from Scripture and thinking about what I read

❑ By just sitting quietly and thinking about God

❑ Other: _____

Public prayer vs. private prayer

All prayer can be classified into two categories: *public prayer* and *private prayer*. Sounds easy enough, but the words don't exactly mean what they say. Public prayer is how the Church describes its official prayer. Therefore private prayer is any unofficial prayer. Public prayer refers to the Church's liturgical prayer, namely the celebration of the Eucharist or any other sacrament, and the celebration of the Divine Office or Prayer of the Hours. In public prayer the Church gathers together in the name of Jesus and unites itself with Jesus, who is represented in most instances by the bishop or priest. In a real sense, it is Jesus who prays and leads the Church in its public prayer.

Suppose twenty people gather together at the parish church to pray the Rosary or to pray the Stations of the Cross. Are these prayers public prayers or private prayers?

These prayers are an example of private prayer because the Rosary and the Stations of the Cross aren't part of the Church's official liturgy. Any prayer that is not a liturgical prayer is an example of private prayer. So it isn't how many people pray together that determines whether a prayer is public or private, it is whether or not the prayer is a liturgical prayer.

As you might expect, a good prayer life includes both public prayer and private prayer. The focus of this chapter is private prayer, while chapter 7 takes a closer look at public prayer.

A Prayer Tradition ✛

Muslim men have an obligation to pray, called salat. *This obligation is fulfilled in two ways: through private prayer and through public prayer. Public prayer for Muslims is the obligatory prayer that is recited five times daily.*

¿ ¿ ¿ Which is it? ? ? ?

Below is a list of many types of prayer. For each prayer, decide whether it is a public prayer or a private prayer. Circle your choice.

Sacrament of Reconciliation	Public	Private
Grace before meals	Public	Private
Celebration of Baptism	Public	Private
A pilgrimage to Lourdes	Public	Private
Benediction of the Blessed Sacrament	Public	Private

Catechism Key

The Holy Spirit, who instructs us to celebrate the liturgy in expectation of Christ's return, teaches us to pray in hope. *Conversely, the prayer of the Church and personal prayer nourish hope in us. . . .* (2657)

Vocal prayer

Think back to your childhood. What was the first prayer you learned? For most Catholic children, the Sign of the Cross was the first prayer they learned. The Sign of the Cross is an example of *vocal* or *formal* prayer. Vocal or formal prayer is a prayer you recite that someone else has composed. The Lord's Prayer and the Hail Mary are more examples of vocal prayers that you probably learned as a small child. This way of praying is probably as old as prayer itself.

There are advantages to using vocal prayers, whether you memorize the words or simply read them out of a prayer book or other source. For starters, it can make praying a little easier. You don't have to think long and hard of what to say or how to say it. It's similar to the old, reliable "Happy Birthday" song. Everyone knows the words and the tune, so it makes it easy to congratulate the guest of honor. Without the song, we'd have to come up with new words and a new tune every time we celebrate someone's birthday.

Also, there are many formal prayers, starting with the Lord's Prayer, that we can't really improve upon. These prayers are classics that have been part of the Church, in some cases, for many centuries.

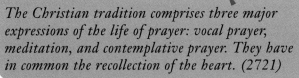

Catechism Key

The Christian tradition comprises three major expressions of the life of prayer: vocal prayer, meditation, and contemplative prayer. They have in common the recollection of the heart. (2721)

There are some problems in saying vocal prayers. First, the words may not express what you are feeling and what you really want to say. There are times that no vocal prayer truly "fits" what you need to express. The second problem is that these prayers often become too much of a habit. You know the words so well that you can say the prayer without thinking about what the words mean. How many times have you said the Sign of the Cross without thinking of what it means? Do you truly think about what you are saying when you say grace before dinner, or are you just waiting to dive into the mashed potatoes? Despite these problems, vocal prayers are always a good way to pray in the right situation.

Many of the psalms in the Bible are prayers written by people just like you, expressing a cry for help or offering praise and thanksgiving for God's goodness. Read Psalms 30 and 71, and then answer these questions:

1. What kind of person do you think wrote each psalm (old, young, rich, poor, famous, ordinary, etc.)?

    30:

    71:

2. What kind of situation do you think each author faced?

    30:

    71:

3. What is each person's attitude toward God?

    30:

    71:

4. What do you think makes each psalm a good prayer?

    30:

    71:

On the spur of the moment

Most people probably pray a *spontaneous* prayer most often. They talk to God just as they would talk to any good friend, expressing their thoughts and feelings, needs and fears, gratitude and sorrow. There is no pattern to follow for spontaneous prayer; just use whatever words come to mind whenever you want to.

This form of prayer can be as short and as quick as "Thanks, God," or "Help me, Lord." Perhaps you might utter a few words to God before you fall asleep or as you brush your teeth in the morning. But don't think spontaneous prayer is limited to five words or less; you may have a long conversation with God if you have a lot to talk about. In fact, many families use spontaneous prayer to express thanks before a meal.

How do you use spontaneous prayer in your daily activities?

_____
_____
_____
_____
_____
_____

Spontaneous prayer is such a popular way to pray because you can do it anywhere, any time. And unlike vocal prayers, very often you find the right words to express what you want to say.

Think about it

Throughout history, people have used *meditation* as a way to pray and communicate with God. It is best described as a combination of thinking about and listening to God. Actually, at times the direct focus of the med-itation may not be on God. You may focus your thinking on a saying or a parable of Jesus, for example, on the sufferings of Jesus or what it really means to love your neighbor as yourself.

But how does meditation qualify as prayer? Are you praying at school when you daydream about life during science class? Unfortunately, no. Daydreaming doesn't qualify as prayer. One thing that makes meditation prayer is your intention. You take some time to think about certain things so that you can discover what God thinks about these same things. You meditate so you can better align your thoughts, values, and actions with God's thoughts, values, and actions.

The second thing that makes meditation prayer is that you spend much of the time *listening*. Unlike "just thinking" (where in a sense you talk to yourself), in meditation the real goal is to hear what God has to say about the matter you are focusing on. In meditation, you always spend some time simply being quiet, not saying anything, but trying to "hear" what God might have to say to you.

Catechism Key

Meditation is a prayerful quest engaging thought, imagination, emotion, and desire. Its goal is to make our own in faith the subject considered, by confronting it with the reality of our own life. (2723)

Often when people meditate they use an aid, such as a Scripture passage or an inspirational reading, to help them focus and to stimulate their thinking. In fact, some people do what is called *meditative reading*.

Ponderin' Peak

43

Here's how it works: Begin by choosing a passage from Scripture or from some other appropriate book. Read very slowly, paying close attention to what you are reading until an idea or an image really grabs you. Then stop reading for a while to think about that idea or image and to listen to God. After a few minutes, when the thoughts stop flowing, begin reading again until another idea or image strikes you. Keep repeating this process throughout the time you set aside for prayer.

Unlike spontaneous prayer, meditation usually requires some planning. Meditation works best when you can establish a routine of when and where you pray. It's important to look for a time and a place that is free of people and activities, which can be distracting. When you're planning this time, set aside at least fifteen minutes to meditate. It usually takes this long just to get settled, to remove all distractions, to relax, and to get focused.

Usually when people start meditating, they spend most of their time thinking and pondering one topic over and over in their mind and spend less time being quiet, listening to God. But as you practice the skill of meditation, you spend more time being quiet and listening and less time thinking. Over time, meditation often leads to *contemplation*.

Scripture Sketch

Open your Bible to the First Letter of Peter, chapter 4, verses 1–11. Take a few quiet moments to do a meditative reading. If things around you are too distracting as you focus, try closing your eyes.

A Prayer Tradition

Zen Buddhists practice meditation to achieve a glimpse of enlightenment about life or satori. *In Japan, Zen Buddhists use the meditation technique of* zazen, *where the Buddhists sit with their eyes open, fixed on a spot on the wall in front of them. The only purpose to this practice is to sit and observe the world as well as one's own thoughts.*

You don't even have to think!

So from meditation often comes contemplation. Contemplation is mostly being quiet and aware of God's presence. You don't talk. You don't think about anything. You just experience God's presence. Have you ever just sat and stared at the flames in a fireplace or at a picture on the wall? Remember how in a sense your mind goes blank? How you lose touch with the things around you though you know they are there? How you get caught up in a feeling of peace and contentment? People might describe this experience as being "spaced-out," dazed. Contemplation is similar to this experience.

Contemplation is a form of prayer where you just "sit and stare at God." You get caught up in a sense of God's presence, in a general feeling of contentment, of peace, of love, or of gratitude—or perhaps all those feelings wrapped together. You become so focused on God that you don't really notice the things going on around you.

Some people move naturally from meditation into contemplation without really planning to. Others make contemplation their goal from the beginning. They use an approach similar to a *centering prayer* to develop their ability to pray in this more focused way. In centering prayer, you calmly and slowly "let go" of your everyday thoughts and the sights and sounds around you. Using your imagination, you "sink" into the center of your being. There, you find God or experience God's presence and simply dwell in that presence. This kind of prayer is a gift, a grace.

Many people may need extra help to get themselves focused and to "center" themselves. These people may choose to use a *mantra*. A mantra is a word or phrase of several syllables that people slowly repeat in their minds over and over. Some people simply keep repeating "Jesus," for example, or "Lord Jesus," or "Lord Jesus, have mercy." This helps people drown out distractions and create a sense of inner peace and quiet so they can better focus their attention on God who brings them into union with him.

Some people seem drawn to this contemplative style of prayer very naturally and find it rather easy. Others find it more natural to spend their time talking to God or meditating. In any case, everyone can experience the prayer of contemplation. If you pray on a regular basis, you will at least occasionally experience moments of contemplation.

A Prayer Tradition

Contemplation is an important part of Zen Buddhism. Having experienced enlightenment through contemplation, the faithful achieve a high level of assurance and grace to face the problems of life. The founder of Zen Buddhism, a Buddhist monk named Bodhidharma (600 C.E.), contemplated on an empty wall for nine years.

The more, the better

As you can see, there are many different ways to pray private prayers. And since all these forms of prayer have the same goal and can help you arrive at that goal, there isn't one that is better than the other. But becoming a person of prayer means learning to use all the different forms of prayer and then choosing which one seems best for you at a given time or in a given situation. When you gather with the community to celebrate the Eucharist, vocal prayer is the usual form your prayer will take. But even the celebration of the Mass allows for some quiet time for private prayer—to meditate and to experience God's presence. In fact, Pope John Paul II has said that we need to have more periods of silent prayer during Mass.

Whatever form of prayer you use most often will improve your practice of other forms. For example, the more you strive to have a strong private prayer life, the easier you will find it to enter into and find meaning in the public prayer of the Church, such as the celebration of the Eucharist. On the other hand, when you regularly attend and enter into public prayer, you'll find you tend to pray more often and more effectively in private.

This is one way I can improve my practice of private prayer:

_____

_____

_____

_____

_____

_____

_____

46

Pause to Pray

Dear Lord,

I hunger and thirst for you.

Show me how to pray in such a way that my hunger and thirst for you can be satisfied.

Teach me to discover your presence in my prayer.

I ask this in the name of Jesus, your Son.

Amen.

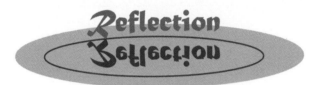

Reflection

Kyle: Mia, wake up! Mom asked me to tell you to set the table.

Mia: Kyle, haven't you ever heard of knocking?

Kyle: Oh, I'm sorry Big Sister. Did I interrupt your beauty sleep?

Mia: Knock it off. I wasn't sleeping.

Kyle: Yeah, right. What were you doing?

Mia: Not that it's any of your business, but I was praying.

Kyle: Oh, I understand. Prayer sometimes puts me to sleep, too.

Mia: Kyle, I told you, I wasn't sleeping. I was meditating.

Kyle: I didn't hear you saying, "Ohmmmm. Ohmmmm."

Mia: I believe you're thinking of a mantra, and it doesn't have to be "Ohmmmm."

It can be any word or phrase, such as "Give me peace, Jesus." By the way, you don't need to use a mantra if you don't want to. It helps some people focus, get rid of distractions.

Kyle: So is this what you do every day while you've got your bedroom door shut?

Mia: I try to. These twenty minutes really help me relax and focus after a long day at school. I enjoy this time when I can just think about things and listen to what God has to say.

Kyle: So you just sit here thinking with your eyes closed. Sounds like math class to me.

Mia: Give me peace, Jesus. Give me peace, Jesus. Give me peace, Jesus.

Kyle: I can take a hint. See ya later. And don't forget to set the table.

Homework

Write a formal prayer that the class could pray together. Pick one of the following occasions, and write your prayer to suit that occasion.

- Beginning of class

- End of class

- Before a quiz

- Before a holiday or vacation

- At the end of the school year

Extra! Extra!

In your own words and with your own thoughts and feelings, please answer the title of this chapter: How should I pray? Your answer should be a paragraph of fifty words or more. Write your answer on page 99 in the appendix.

Am I Too Busy?

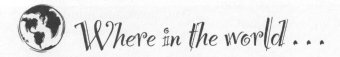

Where in the world . . .

1. When you are at home, where is the best place for you to pray? Why?

_____
_____
_____
_____

2. When you are outside in your neighborhood, where would be a good place to pray? Why would this be a good place?

_____
_____
_____
_____
_____

3. Is there anywhere at school you can pray? Where?

_____
_____
_____
_____

4. At what time of the day do you find it easiest to pray? Why is this a good time to pray?

_____
_____
_____
_____
_____

5. What is your favorite place to pray? Why?

_____
_____
_____
_____

If only I had more time . . .

These days people are always saying they don't have time for this or that. It's true we are very busy people. So when people think about making a commitment to prayer, some question, "How can I find time?" It's not always easy.

There are three types of time we can take during the day for prayer: traditional time, "anytime," and personal time. *Traditional time* is the time during the regular routine of each day and each week when many people turn to God. For example, many people use traditional time for prayer each morning to offer thanks for the new day and to ask for help and guidance during the coming day. At night it is custom to turn once again to God to give thanks, to ask forgiveness, and to seek protection through the night.

Aside from morning prayers and evening prayers, what are some other prayers that you observe during traditional time?

_____

_____

_____

_____

_____

Whatever way you express your thoughts and whatever feelings during traditional prayer time is fine. What's important is that you get into the habit of using your daily routine as a reminder to turn in prayer in order to raise your heart and mind to God. This is a great start to developing a prayer life.

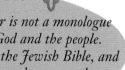

Scripture Sketch

At that same hour Jesus rejoiced in the Holy Spirit and said, "I thank you, Father, Lord of heaven and earth, because you have hidden these things from the wise and the intelligent and have revealed them to infants; yes, Father, for such was your gracious will."
—Luke 10:21

What does this passage tell you about the prayer life of Jesus? What does it tell you about your own prayer life?

_____

_____

_____

A Prayer Tradition

Jewish people believe that prayer is not a monologue but rather a dialogue between God and the people. God talks to the people through the Jewish Bible, and the people respond through prayers, hymns, and preaching.

Anytime, anywhere

But you can pray anytime, can't you? Sure. That's the whole concept of "anytime" prayer. "Anytime" prayer is when you pray whenever you think about it or whenever something comes up that triggers the need or desire to turn to God. Usually "anytime" prayers are short and informal—a spontaneous prayer. Imagine that you are in an airplane on the way to Denver. The entire flight has been very rough and turbulent. You pray to God to ask for the safety of the plane and all its passengers. When the plane lands safely in Denver, you offer a quick thanks to God for taking care of everyone.

Because "anytime" prayers are usually short and spontaneous, you can pray this way anywhere—while walking to the bus stop, when standing in line in the cafeteria, while waiting for a friend at the mall, as you are walking the dog, even while you are cleaning your room.

Catechism Key

It is always possible to pray. . . . *"It is possible to offer fervent prayer even while walking in public or strolling alone, or seated in your shop, . . . while buying or selling, . . . or even while cooking." [St. John Chrysostom, Ecloga de oratione 2: PG 63, 585.] (2743)*

When was the last time you turned to God in an "anytime" prayer. Describe the situation.

_____

_____

_____

_____

_____

But honestly, how often do you think of God as you are standing in line in the cafeteria or as you are waiting for your friend at the mall? Most people probably don't think of God in these situations. So what can we do to remind ourselves to pray to God anywhere and at any time? Some experts suggest that we use little everyday things to remind us to turn a quick thought to God in an "anytime" prayer. Many years ago, for example, the ringing of the church bells at various times during the day helped people remember to say a quick prayer to God. And in the time before cars, people would often build shrines along the roads to remind those walking to stop for a minute to pray. Some people owned medals, crucifixes, and pictures and statues of Jesus and the saints to serve as reminders to pray. All these reminders still work today, by the way!

Actually, just about anything can serve as a reminder to pray. Thinking of tragedy, some people say a prayer every time they hear an emergency siren. Some people who do a lot of driving alone say a short prayer for their safety every time they are stopped at a red light. Whatever the time and wherever the place, these reminders help people turn to God in prayer. Eventually many of these "anytime" prayers may become a habit where you don't need a reminder to help you remember to pray. Then your "anytime" prayer is turned into a traditional time prayer!

List five different things that you see, hear, or do everyday that could serve as a reminder to stop for a few seconds and turn to God in prayer.

1. _____

2. _____

3. _____

4. _____

5. _____

Time for yourself

Establishing some personal time for prayer takes a little extra effort. But in the end this time will probably be the most special prayer in your life. To make this prayer work you have to set aside every day—or at least several times a week—a definite time and place to develop your relationship with God in prayer.

You must do two things to make personal prayer work. First, you need to find a time in your daily routine when you can set aside a few minutes to devote to prayer. Second, you need to find a place where you know you won't be disturbed or distracted by other people or activities.

Take a close look at your daily schedule and decide when you can find fifteen minutes that you can set aside to talk with God. Many people find the fifteen minutes before they go to bed to be the best time. Or if you are an early riser, you may enjoy spending a few quiet moments in prayer before others are up and before the activities of the day start. Finding this time in your schedule may not be as difficult as it sounds. In fact, this time doesn't have to be every day. If some days are busier than others, you may only find free time three or four days a week. That's quite all right.

Once you have the time picked out, the next step is to determine where you can go so you won't be disturbed. Ideally, you should pick a place where you can sit down and be comfortable. The best place to start may be in your own room, unless your little sister or brother is likely to barge in on you. Or, depending upon the weather, you may enjoy talking to God as you enjoy the beauty of nature—sitting under the shade of a tree or lying on the grass. Just remember, don't go to a place where you can be easily distracted.

It's best to try to set up your personal time for prayer at the same time and the same place each day. This helps create a habit of mind in which you easily slip into a prayer mood. You begin to sense this is the time and the place for getting in touch with God.

 *A moment of your time*

Take a few minutes now to review your weekly schedule. Then jot down several times and places that could be reserved as your personal time for prayer. Try to find a time and a place for each day. That way if you end up not having time on Monday, then you have personal prayer time allotted for Tuesday.

Day	Time	Place
Sunday		
Monday		
Tuesday		
Wednesday		
Thursday		
Friday		
Saturday		

In the morning, while it was still very dark, [Jesus] got up and went out to a deserted place, and there he prayed.

—Mark 1:35

What does this passage tell you about the prayer life of Jesus? What does it tell you about your own prayer life?

_____

_____

_____

Reading, thinking, listening

Personal prayer time is more relaxed and more leisurely than other times of prayer. This atmosphere allows you to get more focused and to go deeper into prayer. One approach that works well if you are just developing the habit of personal prayer is using a meditative reading from Scripture. The following is a slight variation of the meditative reading discussed in the last chapter.

1. Choose a Scripture passage. One suggestion is to read a favorite parable or to read the gospel reading for the coming Sunday.

2. Read the passage slowly. Let the words sink in. Perhaps reread the passage if it is short. What phrase jumps out at you? What catches your attention? What idea sticks in your mind? If nothing grabs your attention, reread the passage or turn to another passage until a phrase grabs you.

3. Now reflect on that phrase for a few moments. What does God seem to be saying to you? Don't be in a hurry to answer the question. Be quiet and listen, allowing God to speak to you.

4. After you have listened for a while and have some sense or idea of what God might be saying to you, ask this question: What do I want to say to God in response? Then just talk to God in your own words, sharing your thoughts and feelings at that specific moment. Pause once in a while to let God speak to you. Continue this way until the end of your personal time.

You may be surprised at how quickly your personal prayer time goes after a little practice. In fact, many people choose to extend their personal time for prayer.

A Prayer Tradition

The sacred writings of Islam are compiled into the Quran. The Quran is a collection of the words God spoke to the prophet Muhammad through the angel Gabriel. Because these are the words of God, the Quran cannot be changed in any way and is considered absolute and complete. Therefore, the Quran regulates every aspect of Islamic life, including law, religion, culture, and politics.

So many options

There are other aids to help you begin your personal prayer time. One option is to read a meditation book. Meditation books contain short readings on specific themes and usually include some inspirational thoughts and Scripture quotes. Usually they list some questions related to the theme for you to "discuss" with God.

Some people find that keeping a journal is a good way to pray. All you do is write down your thoughts and feelings as they occur to you. Don't worry about spelling or grammar; just let your thoughts flow onto the paper. Simply pick any topic of concern to you, such as why there is so much suffering in the world or how you can overcome your fears. If you have difficulty choosing a topic, you may want to read a Scripture passage or a meditation book to help you focus your thoughts. Just remember that it's important to include God in your journal. One day you may want to talk to God. Another day you may want to write down what you hear God saying to you.

Aside from being a good way to lift your mind and heart to God, keeping a journal is also an excellent record of your spiritual life. Most people who journal say they find it both interesting and helpful to go back and reread their journal entries from time to time.

Scripture Sketch

And taking the five loaves and the two fish, [Jesus] looked up to heaven, and blessed and broke them, and gave them to the disciples to set before the crowd.
—Luke 9:16

What does this passage tell you about the prayer life of Jesus? What does it tell you about your own prayer life?

_____

_____

_____

_____

The pros and the cons

For over twenty-five years there has been an ongoing battle in the United States over the legality of prayer in public schools. Do you know what the issue is about? How do you feel about the idea of allowing prayer in public schools?

In this activity, the class is going to have a short debate over the issue. Break into two groups. One group will argue for the right to have prayer in public schools. The second group will argue against prayer in public schools.

Each group will prepare a short one-minute opening argument for their position. After each group has presented their opening argument, there will be a short period of time for the groups to question each other.

Pause to Pray

Side 1: O, give thanks to the Lord, for the Lord is good.

All: God's steadfast love endures forever.

Side 2: Give thanks to the God of gods.

All: God's steadfast love endures forever.

Side 1: O, give thanks to the Lord of lords.

All: God's steadfast love endures forever.

Side 2: To the One who alone does great wonders.

All: God's steadfast love endures forever.

Side 1: To the One who by understanding made the heavens.

All: God's steadfast love endures forever.

Side 2: To the One who spread the earth out upon the waters.

All: God's steadfast love endures forever.

Side 1: To the One who made the great lights, the sun to rule over the day and the moon and stars to rule over the night.

All: God's steadfast love endures forever.

Side 2: Give thanks to the God of heaven.

All: God's steadfast love endures forever.

Caryn: Hello?

Juan: Hi, Caryn. It's Juan. I just heard about the car accident. How are you and your mom doing?

Caryn: My leg is really sore yet, but the doctor said the cast should come off in a few weeks. And I should get out of the hospital tonight. Mom's a little sore, too, but at least she's at home. Thanks for asking, Juan.

Juan: So what happened?

Caryn: Apparently the driver who hit us fell asleep at the wheel. It was late, and he had been driving all day.

Juan: Boy, you two were very lucky!

Caryn: I know. I don't think I have ever prayed so hard as I did when we were waiting for the ambulance. I was just so thankful that Mom and the other driver were okay. In fact, I'm making a promise to say a short prayer to God whenever I get into a car.

Juan: You are?

Caryn: Sure. I'm going to ask God to protect the people in my car and to protect all the people we meet as we drive. And when I get back to school, I'm going to say a short prayer for protection as I hobble to the bus stop on my crutches.

Juan: That's a really great idea. I guess it's kind of like how I say a short prayer every time I hear my mom's beeper go off, knowing that there's an emergency at the hospital.

Caryn: Yeah. Hey, maybe your mom's beeper went off the night of my accident.

Juan: When was the accident?

Caryn: Last Sunday night, about 10:00 p.m.

Juan: You know, Mom did get paged Sunday around 10:15 p.m., but she didn't tell me what the emergency was.

Caryn: It must have been our accident. You actually said a prayer for me!

Juan: I did! I never thought that I might actually know the people I pray for when I hear Mom's beeper.

Caryn: That's really neat. Thanks!

Juan: You're welcome. Well, I guess I better go. Mr. Harrison gave us a lot of homework today. Whenever you're feeling better, I'd be happy to bring your homework over to you.

Caryn: Thanks, I hear I'm in for a very long, slow recovery.

Juan: I'll be thinking of you, Caryn. Take care, and I'll give you a call when you get home.

Caryn: Thanks for calling, Juan. Bye.

Juan: Bye.

Homework

Find a quiet place and read slowly Luke 18:18–30. Then reflect on the following three questions.

- What word or phrase catches your attention the most in this passage?

- What might God be saying to you in this passage?

- What do you want to say to God in response?

Now try writing out your reflections as a journal entry.

_____

_____

_____

_____

_____

_____

_____

_____

_____

_____

_____

Extra! Extra!

In your own words and with your own thoughts and feelings, please answer the title of this chapter: Am I too busy? Your answer should be a paragraph of fifty words or more. Write your answer on page 100 in the appendix.

SOS is recognized by ships all over the world as a signal of distress. Therefore, all sailors must learn the skills of how to transmit radio messages using this system of short (·) and long (-) sounds called *Morse code*. Compose a short prayer using the Morse code symbols below to ask God for help.

a · -	f · · - ·	k - · -	p · - - ·	u · · -
b - · · ·	g - - ·	l · - · ·	q - - · -	v · · · -
c - · - ·	h · · · ·	m - -	r · - ·	w · - -
d - · ·	i · ·	n - ·	s · · ·	x - · · -
e ·	j · - - -	o - - -	t -	y - · - -
				z - - · ·

Write the translation of your prayer here:

_____

_____

_____

All alone

You may have heard the local meteorologist on television predict that a major thunderstorm is about to hit your area. If the conditions are just right, a tornado could develop. But what conditions are they talking about? Well, most tornadoes form in the spring or early summer on hot, humid days, usually in the afternoon or early evening. The greatest possibility of a tornado is when the cool, dry air from the north meets the warm, humid air from the Gulf of Mexico, creating a *front*. When a thin strip of thunderstorm clouds form along this front, a tornado could develop. These are the perfect conditions for a tornado to occur.

Just as a tornado must meet specific conditions to occur, prayer has three conditions that should be met as one develops the ability to pray: solitude, silence, and sensitivity.

For starters, don't confuse solitude with loneliness. Being alone is not the same as being lonely. You can be lonely at a party, in the midst of a group of classmates, or living in New York City. You see, it's not the number of people around you that helps cure loneliness; it's the people you know. Loneliness is not a feeling people want to experience.

But people have always sought out solitude. Many times Jesus went in search of this seclusion when he wanted to be alone to pray. In imitation of Jesus, men and women throughout history have sought places of solitude. During the sixth century many monasteries were established exactly for this reason: to spend time praying in solitude. In the same way, many people go off today from time to time to places of solitude called *retreat houses* where they can spend some quiet time in prayer.

How does solitude help you pray? It's fairly obvious. When you go off in solitude, you get away from other people, but you don't get away from God, do you? In fact, because no one else is around to distract you, you can give your full attention to God. That's why people seek solitude when they want to pray—so they can give their full attention to God. And that's why you should never feel lonely even when you are alone.

Let me alone!

Think for a moment of all the times you are alone, not so much by choice but by circumstance. List some of these situations below. Then list some things you may do to distract yourself if you are alone.

Times alone

_____

_____

_____

Things I do to distract myself

_____

_____

_____

Do you think of being alone as a negative experience or a positive experience? Why do you think this way?

_____

_____

_____

Alone, but not lonely

Think back to chapter 5. Do you remember what two things are needed when establishing your habit of personal prayer? The first is to find a time in your daily routine for prayer. The second is to find a place where you won't be disturbed and distracted—a place of solitude where you can give your undivided attention to God.

But also consider this: In our society, most people think being alone is not good, not healthy. Too many people make the mistake of thinking that being alone is being lonely. So if you are like most people, when you are alone you are quick to find something to distract you and to occupy your thoughts. But what would happen if you learned to value this time alone, to view it positively, as an opportunity to get in touch with yourself and with God, like many of Jesus' followers learned to do?

Scripture Sketch

Take a few quiet minutes to read Luke 5:15–16 and to answer the questions below.

• Have you ever felt drawn to seek solitude?

_____

• Do you have a desert place? How did you choose this place?

_____

• Why do you go to your desert place?

_____

You don't have to travel to the desert to experience this solitude. Rather, when the "desert" comes to you and you are forced to be alone, try to see this time as a gift, not as a punishment. Then when life gets hectic for you, you will view this time of solitude as a time to sort things out and to get in touch with what is really important. The fact is, solitude is your friend, not your enemy. Once you see it this way, you will seek out this friend in times of need.

Peace and quiet

Remember, the goal of our prayer is to raise our heart and mind to God. Solitude can help us achieve that goal, but only if the solitude is a time of peace and quiet. Along with solitude, you need silence. And silence, just like solitude, is a difficult thing to achieve for many people. In many ways our society is a noise-addicted society. Chances are you may suffer from that addiction yourself. Is the radio always on when you are in the car? Do you turn on the television or the radio first thing when you get up in the morning or when you get home? Do you fall asleep with the radio or television on? Are you uncomfortable when everything is quiet?

Get the idea? It's not a real solitude if there is noise around you that prevents you from focusing on God. It's not that watching television and listening to music is bad, but it does become a problem if you spend every minute surrounded by noise. How, then, can you get the attention of God and can God get the attention of you?

Actually, external noise is rather easy to control if you decide to do it. After all, you do have the power to turn off the television or radio with the push of a button. You can also physically leave a noisy place to go off to some place where there is no noise.

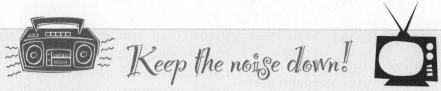

Keep the noise down!

Do you think you're addicted to noise? Before the next class, try the following experiment to see how much noise is in your daily routine.

Choose a day to perform the experiment. Keep track of the noise around you during the day. See if you can go the entire day without listening to the radio, without watching television, without playing video games.

• Were you able to go the entire day without the radio, the television, and video games?

• How difficult was it?

• What did you miss most, if anything?

• When did you find it most difficult?

• Did you find yourself feeling a little nervous, edgy, irritated at times?

• What, if anything, did you learn about yourself from the experiment?

Do you hear voices?

But there is another kind of noise that is more difficult to control than external noise. This noise can be an even bigger obstacle to being able to raise your heart and mind to God. It is internal noise—ideas and feelings, fears and worries, images and daydreams that can rattle around inside your head and occupy all your attention.

Let's say, for example, you set aside twenty minutes of personal time for prayer. You go to your room where you can be alone and experience solitude. To get ready for your prayer, you turn off the radio so you can experience silence. But as you try to focus on the topic of your prayer, you find that worries about tomorrow's test keep popping into your head. When are you going to find time to study? If you don't pass the test, what grades will you need the rest of the semester to pass the class? What will your parents say if you fail the test? With all the internal noise in your head, how can you focus on God?

There is no guaranteed way for quieting this kind of internal noise, but there are a few methods you can try. The first is simply to turn your distractions into topics for your prayer. If you are worried about tomorrow's test, then talk to God about the test—why it is so important to you, what will happen if you fail, and what you like and don't like about being a student. Because God is interested in you, God is interested in everything that is of concern to you.

A second trick for dealing with distracting thoughts is the imaginary-garbage-can method. Before you begin your prayer, close your eyes. Then in your mind, gather all your "noisy" thoughts and place them in an imaginary garbage can. Once your mind is clear of all distracting thoughts, place the imaginary lid on the garbage can. Now you can go on with your prayer. If a "noisy" thought escapes, calmly put it back in the garbage can and place the lid on the can.

Everyone who tries to pray has to deal with some internal noise. Each time you find yourself drifting off in your prayer and paying attention to one of your "noisy" thoughts, simply let it drop and refocus on the topic of your prayer. Clearing your mind of "noisy" thoughts is a skill. With a little practice, you'll find you can experience not just external silence but internal silence as well.

Create an exercise to get rid of "noisy" thoughts. You may wish to pattern your exercise after the garbage can method. Write your method below.

Close your eyes.

_____

_____

_____

_____

_____

A whole new world

Now that you have an understanding of solitude and silence, let's take a few moments to think about what role sensitivity plays in prayer. It all relates to the saying "Stop and smell the roses." In our society many people seem to be so busy rushing around doing things that they forget to take notice of the world around them. They're so intent on what they're doing that they forget how to let nature speak to them.

We can stop and smell the roses, but do the roses talk back to us? Sure. All creation is God's handiwork and everything in nature reflects God or tells us something about God. So whenever we become more sensitive about the world around us and more willing to take time to notice God's work, we realize how everything speaks volumes about God. Being sensitive and alert to our surroundings helps us enjoy a successful prayer life. We understand how God is always present to everyone.

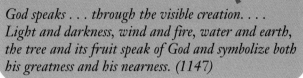

Catechism Key

God speaks . . . through the visible creation. . . . Light and darkness, wind and fire, water and earth, the tree and its fruit speak of God and symbolize both his greatness and his nearness. (1147)

In any case, the whole world—from a dazzling sunset to starlit sky, from a rose to dandelion, from an elephant to an ant—can speak to you of God and serve as a reminder of God's presence, beauty, wisdom, and love—only if you take the time to notice!

Give God a hand

Take a few moments to examine your hand. Look at it carefully. Notice all the characteristics of your hand—the lines and wrinkles, the veins, the fingernails, how it moves, and so forth. The hand is truly amazing. It's a form of communication using sign language and other gestures. It helps blind people read Braille by scanning its fingers over raised dots on paper. Because it is such an important part of our body and it does so many things, there are twenty-seven bones in each hand, or fifty-four in both hands. In total, there are only approximately two hundred bones in our entire body. That means that the bones in our hands make up over one-fourth of the bones in our entire body!

What does your hand reveal to you about the God who "invented" it? Write down below some of your thoughts.

_____
_____
_____
_____
_____

Explain the meaning of the following expression: "Don't take a walk. Let the walk take you."

_____
_____
_____

All rivers are sacred to the Hindu. For the Hindus, each day begins by bathing in a river, saying prayers, washing their mouths, and honoring the sun. Hindus who do not live near a river bathe in a pond, a lake, or a stream. But the Ganges is the most sacred river for the Hindus; they bathe in it for purification.

Sacramental symbols

As you might expect, it is no accident that our sacraments are founded on the belief that things in nature can be powerful aids in communicating to us God's presence and action. Review each of the seven sacramental celebrations. Then list some of the symbols of nature that are an important part of each sacrament.

Baptism _____

Eucharist _____

Confirmation _____

Reconciliation _____

Marriage _____

Holy Orders _____

Anointing of the Sick _____

Scripture Sketch

Take a few minutes to read Psalm 104. After reflecting on the psalm, answer the following questions:

- What does this psalm tell you about God?

- Where should we search for God?

- Has nature ever spoken to you of God the way it seems to have spoken to the writer of this psalm?

It isn't working

Often when people first set aside some personal time for prayer, they complain that nothing seems to happen. First of all, people need to ask what they are expecting to happen. Too often people have mistaken ideas of what to expect from prayer. Some people think they are supposed to experience surges of wonderful feelings or have great flashes of insight that provide immediate answers to their questions.

It's not that we don't experience surges of wonderful feelings or have great flashes of insight, it's just that these experiences don't happen all the time. There will be times in your prayer when the effects are experienced in a more "delayed reaction" kind of way. For example, imagine that you are at Mass on Sunday. The Scripture reading is one you've heard many times before, but today the meaning becomes so clear that you would think it was written just for you. It gives the answer or direction you'd been looking for during prayer but never received. Actually, that is the result of your prayer. It's God speaking to you in response to your prayer. It's just the effect of your prayer happened to take place outside of your personal prayer time.

So even if nothing seems to be happening during your personal prayer time, it doesn't automatically mean there is something wrong with the way you are praying. Many times the effects of your prayer take place at other times and through other means—a comment by a friend, a flash of insight as you are getting ready for school, a special awareness of God's presence and love communicated through the song of a bird or through the sight of a sunset.

Quitters never win, and winners never quit

If you think your expectations are realistic but still feel that your prayer isn't going well, it's perfectly okay to try another approach. But don't give up too soon, especially if you are just trying to establish a habit of personal prayer time. It can take a while to get the hang of prayer and to develop some of the attitudes and skills you need, such as learning how to concentrate and how to shut out internal and external noise. Make sure that if you set aside fifteen minutes of your day for prayer, you use all fifteen minutes. If you cut your prayer time short, you are also cutting yourself short of an incredible experience.

The Hindus consider cows to be sacred. They treat cows with the same respect as they would their mother, believing that every cow is a descendant of Kamadhenu—a heavenly cow with the face of a beautiful woman. It is through the protection of their cows that the Hindus believe they are linked to all that lives.

After you've worked on your personal prayer time, don't be afraid to experiment and try different ways of praying. If you are using Scripture as an aid and it doesn't seem to be helping, try using a book of inspirational readings or meditative readings. Sometimes it helps to change the time you set aside for prayer or the place. But whatever you do, don't give up!

Changing right before your very eyes

If you stay committed and work at becoming a prayerful person, you will gradually begin to experience some definite changes in yourself.

The peace and tranquillity of your prayer time will remain with you throughout each day. So whenever you get upset, you can turn to your inner peace and calmness to get in control, to get more in touch with yourself. You'll also be more patient with others and with yourself. This patience will help you forgive others and accept everyone's faults, including your own.

Not only will you feel more in touch with yourself, but you will also be more in touch with God. You'll be more aware of God's presence and action in your life, not just during prayer time, but at many other times, too. You'll sense that God is close to you, a steady companion and friend.

You'll find that you don't worry as much, especially about the small things in life. In fact, there will be an inner joy and a sense of happiness that surrounds you during the day. It will be easier for you to make decisions because your values and your priorities will be more clear to you, since they will be more in line with God's values and priorities.

You see, prayer really does change you— how you think, how you act, what you say. You can't be best friends with God and not be influenced by God. It's as if God's goodness and wisdom rubs off on you, similar to how you tend to pick up the ideas, attitudes, and mannerisms of your good friends. But with God, you find it easier to drop bad habits and form good ones. Just remember that none of this happens in a day, or even in a month. But if you stick with it, developing a prayer life will change your entire life because it will change you.

From the list below, check whatever results you hope to achieve through prayer. Check as many results as you wish.

❑ Acceptance of others
❑ Awareness of God's presence and actions
❑ Clear values and priorities
❑ Generosity
❑ In touch with yourself
❑ Inner peace
❑ Fewer worries

❑ More decisive
❑ More forgiving of others
❑ More self-control
❑ Patience
❑ Sense of happiness
❑ Sense that God is close

Pause to Pray

The following is a version of Psalm 23, translated for Native Americans by an unknown missioner.

The Great Father Above is a Shepherd Chief;

I am his and I want not.

He hold out to me a rope, and the name of that rope is Love.

And he draws me and he draws me

To a place where the grass is green and the water is not dangerous.

Sometimes my heart is heavy and I fall down,

But he lifts me up and comforts me.

Sometimes he makes the rope into a whip,

But afterwards he gives me his staff to lean on!

He lays his hand on my head and all the "tired" is gone.

His name is Wonderful!

Sometime—it may be soon, it may be a long, long time—

He will lead me into a place between the mountains;

It is dark there, but I will not be afraid

I will not draw back.

For it is in there between the mountains

That the Shepherd Chief will meet me,

And the hunger I have felt along the way

Will be satisfied,

And I will dwell in his house forever.

Jason: So, did you two see Derek last night? He was walking home from school alone again. He looked so lonely.

Penny: I wonder what's wrong with him. We've asked him numerous times if he wanted to walk with us.

Tomas: Maybe he just wants to be alone.

Jason: What do you mean? Why wouldn't he want someone to talk to?

Tomas: I don't know. Perhaps Derek likes to take some quiet time to think.

Penny: I think it's odd. I mean, we are his friends. After all, he enjoys surfing the Internet on Jason's computer, and he and I just went to the movies together last weekend.

Jason: Well, if he doesn't want to be with us, maybe we shouldn't spend time with him.

Tomas: Stop it, Jason. Don't you think you should talk to Derek first?

Jason: No, I think he's made his point clear.

Derek: Hi, guys! What's up?

Tomas: Not too much, but I think Penny has a question she wants to ask you.

Penny: I do? Why doesn't Jason . . .

Jason: No way!

Penny: But . . .

Derek: Penny, tell me what's wrong.

Penny: Derek, are you mad at us, or don't you like us anymore?

Derek: Why would you say that?

Penny: It's just that you never walk home with us, yet you live right next door to Tomas. I thought we were friends and enjoyed spending time together.

Derek: Penny, you guys are my best friends, but walking home is the only time during the day I have to myself to think. In the morning I have to fight with my two older sisters and two younger brothers to get ready for school. Then Dad drives everyone to school. During the day I'm at school. And then in the evening I'm back at home with my family. It's just that nature is so peaceful and calm. It's the only peace and quiet I have during the day.

Jason: I guess I never thought of that, seeing that I have no brothers and sisters.

Penny: Yeah. And I only have one sister, and she's away at college most of the year. Hey, Derek, I'm sorry for getting upset with you.

Derek: That's okay.

Tomas: Well, we better get ready for class, or we'll be late. How about we all meet for lunch at noon?

Penny: Sounds good!

Derek: Okay. I'll meet you all by the vending machines.

Jason: See you then. Now I'm going to go enjoy the peace of study hall. Hope I don't enjoy it so much that I fall asleep!

Homework

Before the next class, "let a walk take you." Rain or shine, take a leisurely walk with no particular destination in mind. Try to be sensitive to the things around you. Immediately after your walk, answer the following questions:

1. What were some of the things you noticed?

2. Were you surprised at the number of things you noticed?

3. Did anything in particular remind you in some way of God?

4. How would you describe the overall experience?

Extra! Extra!

In your own words and with your own thoughts and feelings, please answer the title of this chapter: Do I have the skills? Your answer should be a paragraph of fifty words or more. Write your answer on page 100 in the appendix.

What about Mass?

The Name Game

Take a few minutes to complete the following matching exercise. Match each word in the first column with its definition in the second column.

____ Alb

____ Altar

____ Chalice

____ Chasuble

____ Ciborium

____ Corporal

____ Cruet

____ Paten

____ Purificator

____ Stole

____ Tabernacle

1. The small container used to bring wine or water to the altar during the preparation of the gifts.

2. The cup, usually made of gold or silver, used during the Mass to hold the Blood of Christ.

3. The container used to hold the consecrated hosts for distribution at Communion and to store the Blessed Sacrament after Mass.

4. The long white vestment worn by the priest under the other vestments.

5. The scarf-like vestment the priest drapes around his neck.

6. A small, white cloth placed on the altar and on which the chalice and hosts are placed.

7. The small "cabinet" in which the Blessed Sacrament is kept.

8. A small dish, usually made of gold or silver, used for holding a large host at Mass.

9. The colored outer vestment worn by the priest.

10. The table on which the sacrifice and sacred meal of the Mass is offered.

11. A band of linen used to cleanse the chalice.

Describe your feelings about how Mass is celebrated in your parish.

_____

_____

_____

_____

Don't you get it?

After going to Mass for your entire life, at one time or another you may have felt that Mass is boring and a drag. After all, isn't it the same old thing week after week? Some people feel that they can't relate to what is happening in Mass because the music is outdated and the prayers are too old-fashioned. These people simply don't "get anything out of it."

Why don't these people "get anything out of it"? Perhaps they "don't get it" in the first place. For some reason these people have not yet come to understand the real meaning and value of the Mass. Or they approach Mass with the wrong expectations and the wrong attitude. They go to church expecting "to get something out of it" when, in reality, we are to go to Mass to give something—ourselves. What we "get out" of Mass depends on what we are willing to "put into" it.

The center of our faith

As you know, all life on our planet depends on the sun. The earth revolves around the sun and constantly draws upon its life-giving energy. Without the sun, plants would not be able to produce the oxygen we all need to survive.

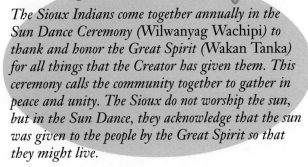

A Prayer Tradition

The Sioux Indians come together annually in the Sun Dance Ceremony (Wilwanyag Wachipi) *to thank and honor the Great Spirit* (Wakan Tanka) *for all things that the Creator has given them. This ceremony calls the community together to gather in peace and unity. The Sioux do not worship the sun, but in the Sun Dance, they acknowledge that the sun was given to the people by the Great Spirit so that they might live.*

So what does our faith revolve around and draw life-giving energy from? The Eucharist is the life-giving center of our faith, especially for our spiritual life and our prayer life. Our spiritual life and all forms of prayer revolve around the Eucharist, from which they draw their energy and life. So trying to grow in faith and to develop a prayer life apart from regular participation in the Eucharist just won't work. Your prayer may start out okay, but it will soon die, just as a plant dies without sunlight.

It is probably no surprise to you to hear that the Eucharist, or Mass, is at the very heart of the mystery of our faith. After all, all seven sacraments look to and flow from the Eucharist. The Sacraments of Baptism and Confirmation,

73

along with Eucharist, initiate us into the Church community. Reconciliation reunites us into the Eucharistic community after we've been separated from the Church by our sin. The Sacraments of Holy Orders and Marriage prepare us to minister within and to the Eucharistic community. And the Sacrament of the Anointing of the Sick draws on the strength of the community to heal us and restore us to full participation.

So in this chapter, you will learn and understand the true nature of the Mass and the meaning and value of the Eucharist. This knowledge will help you participate in the Mass prayerfully. Here are a few points to remember about the Mass that will help you understand it:

- The Mass recalls and re-presents the single most important event in all human history—the sacrificial passion and death, and resurrection of Jesus—the Paschal mystery.

- The Mass is not just a sacrifice but also a holy meal. It is described as a meal in which, by sharing the Body and Blood of Jesus offered to God under the signs of bread and wine, we experience a special communion with Jesus, with God the Father, with the Holy Spirit, and with each other. Jesus is truly present in the Eucharist.

- Jesus is present at the Mass. It is the action and prayer of Jesus that gives the Mass its unique value and special power. And you are invited to join in that action and prayer with Jesus.

- The Mass is the most important thing the Church does. Everything else the Church does flows from and leads back to the Eucharist.

- Through uniting with Jesus at Mass, the Church is able to express a perfect prayer of praise and thanksgiving to God the Father. (*Eucharist* comes from the Greek word for "thanks.")

Think about how important the Mass is, what it represents, how unique it is. When you really begin to understand the true nature of the Mass and what happens at Mass, you will probably approach it with a whole new attitude and a different set of expectations. You will learn to appreciate the value and meaning of the Mass.

Catechism Key

We must therefore consider the Eucharist as:
– thanksgiving and praise to the Father;
– the sacrificial memorial of Christ *and his Body;*
– the presence of Christ by the power of his word and of his Spirit. *(1358)*

Everything's in order——well, not quite

Below the various parts of the Mass are listed in incorrect order. In your group, try to order the parts of the Mass correctly (1–18).

_____ Concluding Rite

_____ Eucharistic Prayer

_____ Gathering Song

_____ General Intercessions

_____ Gospel Reading

_____ Great Amen

_____ Holy, Holy, Holy

_____ Homily

_____ Lamb of God Litany

_____ Penitential Rite/Litany

_____ Preparation of Gifts

_____ Procession

_____ Profession of Faith

_____ Reception of Communion

_____ Sign of Peace

_____ The Lord's Prayer

Scripture Sketch

Open your Bible to Luke 24:13–35. Take a few quiet minutes to read the passage silently. What does this excerpt teach us about the nature and effect of the Eucharist?

_____

_____

_____

_____

Don't just sit back and relax

Too many people approach the Mass as they would a movie or a concert. They mistakenly expect to be entertained. They look to the priest, the choir, the other members of the community to make this time "worth their while." So if the homily isn't inspiring, if the singing is off key, if the decorations aren't fancy and colorful, they feel cheated.

Clearly, that's the wrong approach. The fact is, when you go to Mass, expect to do something! To give something! You should go to Mass to celebrate, not to be entertained. The Mass is about praising and thanking God. You don't go to sit back and watch people; you go to participate, to contribute, to help make things happen. You don't go to listen to the singing; you go to sing. You go to offer yourself—to give your whole self—to God the Father in union with Jesus through the power of the Holy Spirit.

You shouldn't try to measure the Mass in terms of how good you feel during the celebration or after it. Because it is ultimately Jesus who both offers the sacrifice and is also the gift being offered to us, the Mass is always a blessing from God the Father to us.

Can good things happen to you because of your participation in the Mass? Certainly! You can leave Mass more closely united to Jesus, to God the Father, and to the community with whom you celebrated. You can leave renewed, energized, filled with the very life of Christ, and united with the Body of Christ, the Church. After all, the Mass is a celebration. We celebrate the gift of salvation and the new life God the Father gives us in and through Jesus through the power of the Holy Spirit. But these good things are spiritual realities you experience at the level of faith. Just because you can't see, hear, touch, taste, or smell these things, doesn't mean that good things aren't happening to you.

For I received from the Lord what I also handed on to you, that the Lord Jesus on the night when he was betrayed took a loaf of bread, and when he had given thanks, he broke it and said, "This is my body that is for you. Do this in remembrance of me." In the same way he took the cup also, after supper, saying, "This cup is the new covenant in my blood. Do this, as often as you drink it, in remembrance of me." For as often as you eat this bread and drink the cup, you proclaim the Lord's death until he comes.

Whoever, therefore, eats the bread or drinks the cup of the Lord in an unworthy manner will be answerable for the body and blood of the Lord. Examine yourselves, and only then eat of the bread and drink of the cup. For all who eat and drink without discerning the body, eat and drink judgment against themselves.

—*1 Corinthians 11:23–29*

1. What meaning does the Mass have for you?

2. Do you view the Mass the same way Saint Paul does in his letter?

3. How do you view Holy Communion at Mass?

4. How does Saint Paul view Holy Communion?

The basics

Once you have some sense of the importance of the Mass and know what to expect, you are really ready to pray at Mass. All that is left is getting into the habit of doing a few basic things when you are there. These basic things include:

- being part of the community

- uniting your own intentions and actions with those of Jesus

- being open to listen and to receive

- being ready to offer and to give

A Prayer Tradition

In 64 C.E., Nero outlawed Christianity and began the first official persecutions of the Roman Empire. Because their religion was outlawed, Christians were forced to celebrate the Eucharist in secret at people's homes and in the catacombs—a series of underground tunnels. These practices continued in the Roman Empire until 313 C.E., when Emperor Constantine granted the freedom of religion to everyone.

Being part of the community

In simple terms, being part of the community means being willing to join in the activities of the community. As the community gathers, let others know through your actions that you want to be part of the group. Next time you are at Mass, look around the church to see if you can recognize those who don't want to be part of the community. Usually they slouch in the pew with an expression of pain on their faces, as if they are having a root canal at the dentist's office. Often they cross their arms in front of them as a way to keep everyone away. What these people need to do is to smile and to greet others, especially those they don't know. They need to let their voices be heard, in song and in prayer. Whenever it's time to give a community response, they need to speak loudly enough that the people around them can hear their response.

Remember, the celebration is the work of the whole community, and that includes you. (*Liturgy* means "the work of the people.") Together with the community, you are there to praise and thank God. Let your attitude, your voice, and even your posture be one of praise and thanks. This helps others and yourself get into the spirit of the celebration.

This is how I can show that I enjoy being part of the community at Mass:

_____

_____

_____

_____

_____

Uniting your intentions and actions with those of Jesus

Since the Mass is the action and prayer of Jesus, we must strive to recognize Jesus' act of self-giving obedience and love for God in order to enter into the Mass. At Mass, there are many signs of Jesus' presence and action—the words and actions of the priest, the Lectionary and the proclamation of the Word, the altar, the community, and, of course, the signs of bread and wine through which Jesus is present as our sacrifice and our spiritual food. If often helps if you take a moment after arriving at church to focus on Jesus and to consciously align your attitude with Jesus' desire to give himself to God the Father in obedience and love.

Scripture Sketch

Read in your Bible each of the following descriptions of the Last Supper.

- Matthew 26:17–30
- Mark 14:12–26
- Luke 22:14–22
- 1 Corinthians 11:23–26

Compare the stories. In what ways are they all alike? In what ways are they all different? How important do you think the differences are? Why?

Being open to listen and to receive

Throughout the Mass there are many times we are called to open ourselves and allow God to speak to us, such as during the reading of the Scriptures and during the homily.

Not only are we asked to listen to God speak, but we are asked to respond by opening ourselves up and receiving some of the many gifts of God. Several times during the Mass, God offers forgiveness to everyone. We are also offered the gift of peace from God and from the community. Hold yourself open to receive these gifts. At Communion we are offered the gift of Jesus truly present in the Eucharist. Open yourself to receive Jesus, and welcome Jesus into your body, your heart, and your life. We are offered communion and friendship with all those present in the community. Welcome them into your life as well.

Being ready to offer and to give

Not only are we called to open ourselves to receive, but we are also called to open ourselves to give. Be ready to offer yourself during the preparation of the gifts—your strengths and weaknesses, your successes and failures, your needs and gifts—so that they may be made holy and acceptable to God. Be ready to have this gift of self united and transformed by the Holy Spirit into Jesus' own gift of self, just as the bread and wine are transformed into his Body and Blood. Be ready to give yourself, with Jesus, to God the Father in a sacrifice of praise and thanksgiving. Be ready to give yourself to others in a gift of forgiveness and peace. And be ready to give yourself to Jesus just as he gives himself to you in Communion.

This is what I can offer of myself to God at Mass this week:

_____
_____
_____
_____
_____
_____
_____
_____
_____

The end results

Your personal prayer outside of Mass plays an important role in your ability to enter into the Mass. For example, if you listen to God well during your personal prayer, then you will find it much easier to listen to God speaking to you during Mass. If during your personal prayer you grow in friendship with Jesus, then it will be easy for you to experience his presence and to unite with his intentions and actions at Mass. If your personal prayer puts you in touch with your needs and weaknesses, it becomes very natural to offer them to God at Mass and to ask for the help you need. If your personal prayer makes you more aware of how generous God is, then offering thanks to God at Mass will be natural for you.

The reverse works as well. The more deeply you enter into the mystery of the Mass and experience communion with the Trinity, the more enriched your personal prayer will be. You'll find that you become more aware of God's presence in your daily life. Because of this awareness, you'll be more likely to remember to pray. And when you do take some time to pray, you will find that you can focus on God more quickly. Your personal prayer will become more energized and fruitful.

In the same way, the closer you grow with the community as you join them in the celebration and share communion with them, the closer the bond will be with the community when you are outside of Mass. Because of this closer bond, you'll find that you are more sensitive to the needs of the community and are eager to help whenever you can. You will also feel more free to turn to them for help and support. You will appreciate their gifts, talents, and good works, and will be more willing yourself to join in carrying out the works of the gospel.

Corporal Works of Mercy

1. Feed the hungry.

2. Give drink to the thirsty.

3. Clothe the naked.

4. Shelter the homeless.

5. Visit the sick.

6. Visit the imprisoned.

7. Bury the dead.

Write a prayer based on the seven corporal works of mercy.

Spiritual Works of Mercy

1. Counsel the doubtful.

2. Instruct the ignorant.

3. Admonish the sinner.

4. Comfort the sorrowful.

5. Forgive injuries.

6. Bear wrongs patiently.

7. Pray for the living and the dead.

Write a prayer based on the seven spiritual works of mercy.

Pause to Pray

Leader: Jesus, deep in our hearts we know that religious ceremonies are very important in our lives. They remind us that you are always with us pointing the way to God.

Right Side: When we are tempted not to go to Mass, not to pray, and not to receive the sacraments, remind us of our need for you.

Left Side: It is through these experiences that we encounter you in a special way. As a community of believers, we express our faith with you in our midst.

Right Side: Help us to remember that we, too, have something to offer every time we go to Mass. We can reach out to those around us and share our faith and our prayers.

Left Side: This is very hard for us, Jesus, because we like to be entertained. The Mass can be hard work, too hard unless you help us.

Right Side: Above all, help us to remember that every time we gather at Mass, every time we pray together, we do it to remember you.

All: Amen.

Dad: Keely, it's time to get up!

Keely: (sigh, grumble)

Dad: Come on. I already let you sleep in fifteen minutes. If you don't get up now, you're going to be late for Mass.

Keely: Dad, can't I just skip Mass this week? I was out baby-sitting until midnight last night.

Dad: I know. That's why we decided to go to eleven o'clock Mass with you.

Keely: But I don't want to go. I'm just going to sleep through it anyway.

Dad: Keely, I think nine and a half hours of sleep is plenty for anyone, including teenagers.

Keely: Dad, please, just this once let me stay home. I never get anything out of Mass anyway.

Dad: Why don't you?

Keely: I don't know.

Dad: Could it be because you never put anything into Mass?

Keely: It's too early for this, Dad. What do you mean?

Dad: Well, I noticed last week you were playing with the Carlson's baby in front of us. And I've noticed many times how you flirt with Thom from your class.

Keely: Dad!

Dad: Keely, what I'm saying is that you can't expect to get anything out of Mass unless you are willing to pay attention, listen, and participate.

Keely: I guess I could try a little harder. It's not that my faith isn't important to me. I mean I've been really trying to take some time out of my day to pray.

Dad: I know, and I'm really proud of you. How is it going?

Keely: Okay. Sometimes it's hard to concentrate, though. I have a hard time focusing my thoughts on God.

Dad: Just like you do in Mass?

Keely: I guess so.

Dad: You know, I bet if you work at concentrating and focusing on God at Mass, it will help you concentrate and focus on God during your prayer time.

Keely: Yeah, maybe that would work.

Dad: Sure it would. Now, you better hurry up and get ready. We have to leave in twenty-five minutes.

Keely: Oh, Dad! You should have woke me earlier!

Homework

> *Meditate daily on the words of your Creator. Learn the heart of God in the words of God, that your soul may be kindled with greater longings for heavenly joys.*
>
> —*Pope Saint Gregory I*

Turn to page 101 in the appendix. On the calendar, fill in the month, year, and dates for the coming month. (You will probably need to refer to a yearly calendar for the dates.) For each day of the month, cite a passage from Scripture that you can use as your daily prayer.

Extra! Extra!

In your own words and with your own thoughts and feelings, please answer the title of this chapter: What about Mass? Your answer should be a paragraph of fifty words or more. Write your answer on page 100 in the appendix.

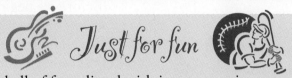

Just for fun

See if you can match each hall of fame listed with its correct city.

____ National Cowboy Hall of Fame

____ Motorsports Museum and Hall of Fame

____ International Hockey Hall of Fame and Museum

____ Gospel Music Hall of Fame and Museum

____ National Baseball Hall of Fame and Museum

____ International Swimming Hall of Fame

____ Rock and Roll Hall of Fame and Museum

____ National Italian American Sports Hall of Fame

____ Pro Football Hall of Fame

____ National Softball Hall of Fame

____ International Frisbee Hall of Fame

____ Rocky Mountain Motorcycle Museum and Hall of Fame

____ National Sprint Car Hall of Fame and Museum

____ World Kite Museum and Hall of Fame

____ National Bowling Hall of Fame and Museum

____ The American Police Hall of Fame and Museum

____ National Polish American Sports Hall of Fame and Museum

____ U.S. Croquet Hall of Fame

____ International Boxing Hall of Fame

____ National Soccer Hall of Fame

a. Colorado Springs, Colorado

b. Fort Lauderdale, Florida

c. Miami, Florida

d. Palm Beach Gardens, Florida

e. Arlington Heights, Illinois

f. Knoxville, Iowa

g. Detroit, Michigan

h. Detroit, Michigan

i. Lake Linden, Michigan

j. Novi, Michigan

k. St. Louis, Missouri

l. Canastota, New York

m. Cooperstown, New York

n. Oneonta, New York

o. Canton, Ohio

p. Cleveland, Ohio

q. Oklahoma City, Oklahoma

r. Oklahoma City, Oklahoma

s. Long Beach, Washington

t. Kingston, Ontario, Canada

Prayer Hall of Fame

Have you ever visited one of the many halls of fame in the United States? Just about every sport has one—football, baseball, softball, hockey, soccer. And just about every form of music has one, including the Country Music Hall of Fame, the Gospel Music Hall of Fame, and the Rock and Roll Hall of Fame.

The purpose of a hall of fame is basically the same for each organization. A hall of fame serves as a showcase to honor the people who did the most for a particular sport or activity. It also serves as a museum to preserve and recall the great events and special memories associated with the sport or activity, such as Babe Ruth's bat or Elvis Presley's guitar.

The Church has no hall of fame for prayer, but in this chapter, you'll be touring the Crossroads Prayer Hall of Fame. On the tour, you will see some of the great traditions and forms of prayer that developed in the Church over the years. Unfortunately, the time for our tour has been cut short, so you will not be seeing all the prayer traditions in the Prayer Hall of Fame. But the prayers you will be examining are an excellent example of the rich tradition you have inherited from your ancestors in faith.

Before we begin, let's preview what you'll be seeing on the tour. The Crossroads Prayer Hall of Fame isn't exactly a museum. Though some of the forms of prayer that you'll be seeing were more popular years ago than they are today, none of these prayers are outdated. In fact, many of the prayers you'll be examining are timeless and work well for every generation. You can learn something about prayer from everything in the hall of fame. So, if you are ready, we can begin the tour. Please follow close behind, and don't wander away from the tour.

What prayers would you include in the Prayer Hall of Fame?

_____
_____
_____
_____
_____
_____

The Rosary

Our first stop on the tour is the Rosary. Dating back to the fifteenth century, the rosary still functions as an aid to prayer today. Consisting of a crucifix and a string of beads, the rosary looks much like a necklace. In fact, in some cultures it is custom to wear a rosary around the neck as a sign of devotion. The beads on the rosary are divided into decades—groups of ten small beads separated by a larger bead. The typical rosary has five decades plus the crucifix, although there are some larger rosaries that have fifteen decades, a total of 150 beads.

A Prayer Tradition ✠

A common practice in Islam is tasbíh, *the act of praising Allāh through use of rosary beads. Since the ninth century, Muslims have used the tasbīh to remember the "beautiful names of God" or to count phrases repeated again and again during ceremonial remembrances.*

The Rosary developed in monasteries, where it was custom for the monks and nuns to pray the Liturgy of the Hours each day. This meant gathering all the people together, including monks, nuns, and lay brothers and sisters, to read and chant fifty psalms throughout the course of the day. But often the lay brothers and sisters were unable to read. Because they couldn't join in reading and chanting the psalms, someone came up with the idea of using a set of fifty beads (one for each of the fifty psalms) for the lay brothers and sisters to count when reciting the Lord's Prayer and the Hail Mary.

That simple device used to count Hail Marys has developed, with relatively few changes, into one of the most popular and widely used prayers in the history of the Church. The custom of praying the Rosary moved out of the monasteries and began to be used by all people. Eventually, the beads were formed into the decades we recognize today. Each decade was then assigned an event or mystery associated with the lives of Jesus and Mary. As people pray the decade, they reflect on the mystery assigned to it. There are a total of fifteen mysteries of the Rosary, but ordinarily only a third of the Rosary, called a *chaplet*, is said at one time. The chaplets include the Joyful Mysteries, the Sorrowful Mysteries, and the Glorious Mysteries. For each chaplet of the Rosary, the faithful recite one Lord's Prayer, ten Hail Marys, and the Trinity Prayer.

Given Mary's special role in the life of Jesus and of the Church, she has always had a unique place in the heart of the Church and in the prayer life of the people. Eventually the Rosary became regarded as Mary's prayer, as a form of devotion especially pleasing to the Mother of Jesus. Once that happened, praying the Rosary became almost as important a part of the prayer life of the Church as the Mass itself. It was prayed by all age groups everywhere in the world.

Because it is such a simple prayer for children and adults to learn, the Rosary has been a popular prayer for many years. But for various reasons, the Rosary has lost some of its popularity in recent years. Nevertheless, it remains a very effective way to raise one's heart and mind to God, either as a group or as a prayer to meditate on alone. It can be as useful a prayer form for you today as it was for the monks, nuns, and lay brothers and sisters who first used it in the twelfth century.

Now, let's continue our tour as we move on to the next exhibit.

In the first column, the events of the mysteries of the Rosary are listed. In the second column, the Scripture passages that refer to the mysteries are listed. Look up each Scripture passage and match it with the correct event.

Joyful Mysteries

____ The annunciation

____ The visitation

____ The birth of Jesus

____ The presentation in the temple

____ Mary and Joseph find Jesus in the temple

Sorrowful Mysteries

____ The agony in the garden

____ The scourging of Jesus

____ The crowning with thorns

____ Jesus carries his cross

____ Jesus dies on the cross

Glorious Mysteries

____ The resurrection

____ The ascension

____ The Holy Spirit is sent upon the apostles

____ The assumption of Mary

____ Mary is crowned queen of heaven and earth

1. Psalm 16:9–10

2. Matthew 28:1–10

3. Mark 14:32–42

4. Mark 15:15

5. Mark 15:33–41

6. Luke 1:26–36

7. Luke 1:37–56

8. Luke 2:1–18

9. Luke 2:22–35

10. Luke 2:41–52

11. John 19:2–3

12. John 19:16–17

13. Acts 1:6–11

14. Acts 2:1–4

15. Revelation 12:1

Catechism Key

Besides sacramental liturgy and sacramentals, catechesis must take into account the forms of piety and popular devotions among the faithful. The religious sense of the Christian people has always found expression in various forms of piety surrounding the Church's sacramental life, such as the veneration of relics, visits to sanctuaries, pilgrimages, processions, the stations of the cross, religious dances, the rosary, medals, [Cf. Council of Nicaea II: DS 601; 603; Council of Trent: DS 1822.] etc. (1674)

The Stations of the Cross

The next stop on the tour is the Stations of the Cross, often called *the Way of the Cross*. The Stations of the Cross revisit the last hours of Jesus' life, especially the painful journey through the streets of Jerusalem to Calvary. The practice of retracing Jesus' last hours began when the early Crusades made it possible for Christians to safely visit Jerusalem again. Pilgrims to Jerusalem would retrace what was considered to be the actual route Jesus walked along on the Way of the Cross. They would stop to pray at fourteen spots called *stations* where they believed certain events related to Jesus' passion and death took place.

Not everyone could travel to Jerusalem. And in time, it became once again too dangerous to travel to Jerusalem. So in the fourteenth century, the Franciscans promoted the custom of placing fourteen wooden crosses along the walls of a church or along a road. Each cross symbolized one of the stations in Jerusalem. People could then pray the stations in the way the pilgrims once did in the Holy Land.

In a short time, artists began to paint pictures or carve statues depicting the event of each station. And composers began to write prayers for the people to say and hymns for them to sing as they moved from station to station. These aids greatly helped the people as they meditated on Jesus' sufferings and death.

Today, virtually every Catholic church in the world has the stations of the cross depicted on its walls. In many parishes, it became custom to pray the Stations of the Cross as a community, especially on the Fridays during Lent, although the Stations of the Cross can be prayed alone. The Stations of the Cross is a wonderful way to meditate on the great love Jesus showed us through the suffering he accepted to free us from sin.

As you can see, the Stations of the Cross deserves a special place in the Prayer Hall of Fame. If you'll follow me, we can move on to the next exhibit.

The Stations of the Cross

First station: Jesus is condemned to death.

Second station: Jesus is made to carry his cross.

Third station: Jesus falls for the first time.

Fourth station: Jesus meets Mary, his mother.

Fifth station: Simon, the Cyrenian, helps Jesus carry his cross.

Sixth station: Veronica wipes the face of Jesus.

Seventh station: Jesus falls the second time.

Eighth station: Jesus speaks to the daughters of Jerusalem.

Ninth station: Jesus falls the third time.

Tenth station: Jesus is stripped of his garments.

Eleventh station: Jesus is nailed to the cross.

Twelfth station: Jesus dies on the cross.

Thirteenth station: Jesus is taken down from the cross.

Fourteenth station: Jesus is laid in the tomb.

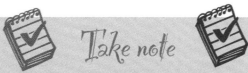

Do you know where the stations of the cross are located in your parish church? In the space below, draw a simple floor plan of your church and put an ✕ in each place you think a station is located. By each ✕, number the station (1–14).

How would you describe the stations of the cross in your parish?

_____

_____

_____

_____

_____

The word *novena* comes from the Latin word *novem*, meaning "nine."
So when we pray a novena, what significance might the number "nine" have?

_____

_____

Novenas

In this exhibit of the Prayer Hall of Fame, you will be introduced to the novena. A novena is a period of prayer that lasts for nine days in a row, or if said once a week, that lasts for nine weeks in a row. The significance of the number "nine" originates from the nine days between Christ's ascension and Pentecost, the period when Mary and the apostles waited for the coming of the Holy Spirit.

The novena began in the seventeenth century with the custom of praying special prayers for the nine days immediately following a person's death. These prayers petitioned God to allow the soul of the deceased to rest in peace. Gradually, the practice of a novena of prayer became a popular way to pray for any favor or on any occasion.

✦ A Prayer Tradition

The Hopi Indians in northeastern Arizona practice a sacred ceremony called the snake dance to pray for rain and good crops. The ceremony is held each August and lasts for nine days. The reason it is called the snake dance is because near the end of the ceremony, the Snake priests dance with live rattlesnakes in their mouths.

The common element in all novenas, then, is the length of the devotion, usually nine days. What form the prayer takes during those nine days varies with the purpose of the novena. For example, it became custom to prepare for a saint's feast day with a novena of prayers. The prayers usually recalled the saint's work and petitioned the saint to intercede to God for protection or for a particular favor. Since many saints became patrons known for bestowing protection or a special gift, the novena of prayers often focused on asking for that gift or for protection.

Sometimes parishes will hold public novenas in honor of a particular saint, especially for the patron saint of the parish. Members of the community gather at a set time each of the nine days before the feast to recite prayers, meditate, and sing hymns. This is still a common practice in some parishes and in some countries. Remember, even if a novena is said with the community, it is still a form of private prayer.

An individual may choose to say a novena as part of his or her daily prayer. The focus of the novena doesn't have to be on a saint and that saint's work. Instead, you may choose to focus on an occasion, a special intention, or any concern. Most importantly, praying the same prayer for nine days helps people develop a habit of praying by serving as a reminder.

Novenas are still popular in some parishes but, like the Rosary, are not practiced as much today as in years past. In some parishes and communities today, novenas are a very important part of their tradition. For example, the Hispanic community celebrates an Advent novena nine days before Christmas Eve called *Las Posadas*, meaning "the inns." In this novena, members of the community reenact Mary and Joseph's search for lodging in Bethlehem, visiting the homes of various parishioners. After approaching three to five homes and being turned away each time, Mary and Joseph finally find lodging at a home decorated with lighted candles set inside paper bags that line the paths leading to the door. The people are then invited into the home for a small celebration. For many Hispanics in the United States, Los Posadas signifies their own lives when they came to America, a strange land, and were not always offered hospitality.

Let's move on to the next exhibit of the tour to see another way people often pray to the saints.

Did you receive at baptism the name of a saint? If so, give as much information as you know about your patron saint—what he or she did, where he or she lived, his or her feast day, etc.

_____
_____
_____
_____
_____
_____

Devotions to the saints

Though the novena is one of the more common devotions to the saints, praying to the saints is a popular form of prayer as well. As you know, saints are recognized by the Church as special friends of God, people who showed great faith, goodness, and courage in living the gospel during their lifetime. Because of their extraordinary lives and works, the Church honors them with special feasts. And because they are special friends of God, we often turn to the saints when we seek help or protection.

Sure, all prayer is ultimately aimed at God, and most often we address God directly. But since the first century, it has been a custom of the Church to ask the saints to intercede to God for us. Just about every saint is considered a patron, known for a special gift, ability, or quality related to his or her life. For example, Saint Anthony is the patron of lost objects, to whom we often turn for help in finding something that is lost. Some saints are patrons of specific occupations. And there are even patron saints for nations all over the world. Mary, the Immaculate Conception, is the patroness of the United States.

Now, we are nearing the end of the tour. If you'll follow me, we have one more exhibit to visit.

Patron Saint of . . .

Try to match each saint with what he or she is the patron saint of.

____ Our Lady of Grace	a. Animals
____ Saint Apollonia	b. Cancer patients
____ Saint Blaise	c. Carpenters
____ Saint Cecilia	d. Charitable societies
____ Saint Francis	e. Dentists
____ Saint Francis de Sales	f. France
____ Saint Joan of Arc	g. Greetings
____ Saint Joseph	h. Ireland
____ Saint Jude	i. Journalists
____ Saint Matthew	j. Lost causes
____ Saint Monica	k. Mothers
____ Saint Patrick	l. Motorcyclists
____ Saint Peregrine	m. Musicians
____ Saint Thomas Aquinas	n. Schools
____ Saint Valentine	o. Sore throat
____ Saint Vincent de Paul	p. Tax collectors

Prayer of Saint Francis

Lord, make me an instrument of your peace.
Where there is hatred, let me sow love,
Where there is injury, pardon,
Where there is doubt, faith.
Where there is despair, hope,
Where there is darkness, light,
Where there is sadness, joy.
Grant that I may not so much seek
to be consoled as to console;
to be understood as to understand,
to be loved as to love;
for it is in giving that we receive,
it is in pardoning that we are pardoned,
and it is in dying that we are born to eternal life.
Amen.

Rewrite the Prayer of Saint Francis in your own words. You many choose to take a few ideas from the prayer and expand upon them instead of rewriting the entire prayer.

Liturgy of the Hours

Welcome to the last exhibit in the Crossroads Prayer Hall of Fame. The *Liturgy of the Hours*, also known as the *Divine Office*, is an important and age-old part of the Church's public or official prayer. The first monks and nuns in the monasteries to pray the Liturgy of the Hours believed that their main duty was to praise God. So they established set times each day to chant psalms, read Scripture, and sing hymns—all in praise of God. These times set the rhythm of their day. Everything else they did revolved around their work of praising God.

This practice of monastic prayer eventually became a very precise form. Specific psalms were said at specific times, and certain hymns and prayers became a requirement for the Liturgy of the Hours. Eventually the prayer came to reflect the liturgical seasons and would change accordingly, for example, during Lent and during the Easter season.

The names of the hours for prayer developed into the following:

- *Matins and Lauds*—very early in the morning; morning praise

- *Prime*—around six A.M., before beginning the work of the day

- *Terce*—around nine A.M.

- *Sext*—around noon

- *None*—around three P.M.

- *Vespers*—evening praise

- *Compline*—a communal night prayer just before retiring

Eventually this form of prayer moved out of the monastery. It became the duty of every ordained priest, not just monks and nuns, to pray the Divine Office each day in private. It also became the custom for some of the laity to pray the Divine Office, especially as shorter, simpler forms of the prayer became available. Sometimes people in the community would join the monks and the nuns in the monastery church to pray parts of the Divine Office, usually Vespers or Compline. In time, parishes began to hold a Vespers service for the community on Sunday evenings.

Because the Liturgy of the Hours is one of the Church's official or public prayers, it continues to be prayed in monasteries today as one of the chief duties of the monks and nuns. All priests, though not required in the same way to pray the full Divine Office each day, are required to pray it in a shortened form. And it is becoming more popular among the laity again, especially in the various updated, shorter and simpler forms. Today, many parishes continue to hold Vespers services, also, at least on special feast days.

As one of the oldest continuous forms of prayer in the Church, the Liturgy of the Hours has earned a special place in our Prayer Hall of Fame.

Catechism Key

The Church invites the faithful to regular prayer: daily prayers, the Liturgy of the Hours, Sunday Eucharist, the feasts of the liturgical year. (2720)

That concludes our tour

Well, thank you for joining us on this tour of the Crossroads Prayer Hall of Fame. There are many other exhibits that we didn't have time to explore, such as the Pilgrimage exhibit, the Rogation Days exhibit, the Forty Hours Devotion exhibit, the Litany exhibit, and the Perpetual Adoration exhibit. Hopefully through this abbreviated tour, you understand that the Catholic Church has a rich prayer tradition. Although parts of this prayer tradition date back many centuries, some prayers never go out of date, such as the Rosary and the Stations of the Cross. They are as effective in raising our hearts and minds to God as they were when our ancestors in faith first developed them. So, besides praying the ways you already know, you may want to explore some of these other forms of prayer, too.

Not only are we at the end of our tour of the Crossroads Prayer Hall of Fame, but we are also at the end of our study of prayer. We've explored the nature of prayer, its purposes, the common forms it takes, and some tips and suggestions for getting started and becoming effective at prayer. From this study, we hope you are now convinced how important prayer is for everyone and how we should all work at developing our prayer life. The following poem does a very good job of explaining prayer:

> God said, "Come to the edge."
>
> "We can't. We're afraid," they answered.
>
> "Come to the edge," God repeated.
>
> "We can't. We're afraid," they answered.
>
> "Come to the edge," God urged one more time.
>
> And they came.
>
> And God pushed them.
>
> And they flew!

May God push you, also.

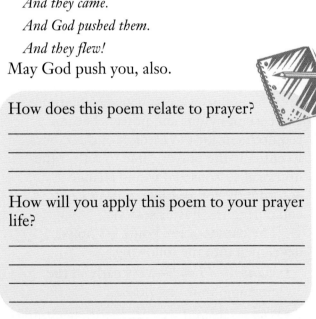

How does this poem relate to prayer?

_____

_____

_____

How will you apply this poem to your prayer life?

_____

_____

_____

_____

94

Pause to Pray

Lord, all your works show your glory.

We stand in wonder and awe

when we behold them—

the sun and moon and stars,

the mountains and oceans,

the mighty beasts and delicate flowers.

Therefore, we join in the chorus of all creation

*as we sing your praises and give thanks for your generosity
and love.*

*In the name of Mary, the mother of Jesus, we ask that you
send upon us*

*your Spirit of prayer so we can walk with you all the days
of our lives. Amen.*

God: Are you proud of your tradition?

Me: What a funny question, God. Of course, I am proud of my tradition. Why do you ask?

God: I don't see you taking it very seriously. You seem intent on discovering new answers to all of life's questions instead of weighing the experience of your forebears. Why?

Me: God, life is new today—new questions, new problems, new technologies, new relationships. Tradition is for the museums. We are building a whole new world.

God: Ah, that is what I thought you might say. There is nothing to be learned in museums, then?

Me: Not much, God. Oh, I suppose there are a few insights but think of our world with its computers, space shuttles, television, the women's movement, nuclear power, and on and on.

God: And people?

Me: Well yes, of course, people.

God: They are still much the same, aren't they?

Me: I suppose they are, deep down inside.

God: That is why tradition is a great teacher. I don't mean that you should quit striving to improve, but I do want you to take tradition seriously as you confront your modern world. Remember, every generation thinks it is coping with a modern world. Won't your experiences have value for your children and grandchildren?

Me: I hope they will. I want to leave the world better than I found it.

God: So did your grandparents and theirs before them. Tradition is a gold mine of insight, wisdom, and vitality. Use it well.

—Excerpt from Prayer-talk *by William V. Coleman (Notre Dame, IN: Ave Maria Press, 1983), pages 90–91.*

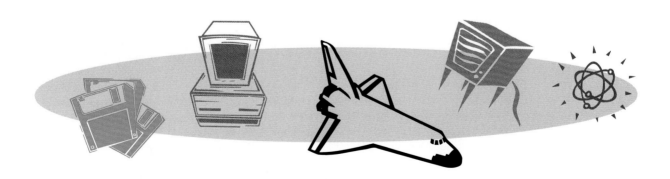

Homework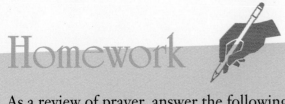

As a review of prayer, answer the following questions.

1. Give a simple definition of prayer.

_____

_____

2. What are the five traditional purposes of prayer?

_____

_____

3. What is the difference between public and private prayer?

_____

_____

4. In what ways does God answer all prayers?

_____

_____

5. Explain the difference between meditation and contemplation.

_____

_____

6. Explain "traditional time," "personal time," and "anytime" as they apply to prayer.

_____

_____

7. How are solitude, silence, and sensitivity important when developing a prayer life?

_____

_____

8. What are the two common mistakes people make regarding the Mass that prevents them from being able to enter into it prayerfully?

_____

_____

Extra! Extra!

In your own words and with your own thoughts and feelings, please answer the title of this chapter: Are there other ways to pray? Your answer should be a paragraph of fifty words or more. Write your answer on page 100 in the appendix.

Appendix I

Have All the Questions Been Answered?

Extra! Extra!

1: Who will listen to me?

_____
_____
_____
_____
_____

2: What should I say?

_____
_____
_____
_____
_____
_____

3: What's the answer?

_____
_____
_____
_____
_____
_____

4: How should I pray?

_____
_____
_____
_____
_____

5: Am I too busy?

_____

_____

_____

_____

_____

6: Do I have the skills?

_____

_____

_____

_____

_____

7: What about Mass?

_____

_____

_____

_____

_____

8: Are there other ways to pray?

_____

_____

_____

_____

_____

Saturday		Friday		Thursday		Wednesday		Tuesday		Monday		Sunday	
☐		☐		☐		☐		☐		☐		☐	
☐		☐		☐		☐		☐		☐		☐	
☐		☐		☐		☐		☐		☐		☐	
☐		☐		☐		☐		☐		☐		☐	
☐		☐		☐		☐		☐		☐		☐	

Prayer Cards

When you want to praise God, read Psalm 148 or Psalm 150.

When you are in search of a friend, read John 13:34–35 or John 15:12–17.

When you want to be free of all your worries, read Matthew 6:25–34.

When you need the strength to forgive another, read Matthew 5:38–48.

When you have done something wrong, read Matthew 5:21–26 or Luke 17:1–4.

When you are sad and depressed, read Psalm 1 or Sirach 30:21–27.

When you are called to help another, read Luke 10:25–37.

When you need someone to trust, read Psalm 27, Psalm 62, or Psalm 145:14–21.

When you are in need of God's guidance, read Psalm 25 or Psalm 119:33–40.

When there is conflict in your life, read Psalm 77.

When you seek protection in God, read Psalm 31:1–9, 20–25.

When you are called to work for justice, read Isaiah 42:1–9.

When you are in need of a guardian angel, read Exodus 23:20–22 or Psalm 91:9–13.

When you forget how to be a disciple of Jesus, read Luke 14:25–33.

When you get upset with another person, read John 13:34–35 or 1 Corinthians 13:1–8

When you need God's forgiveness, read Psalm 32, Psalm 51, or Psalm 130.

When you are jealous of another, read Philippians 2:1–41 or Peter 5:5–11.

When material things become most important to you, read Psalm 49 or Luke 16:19–31.

When you think you are better than someone else, read Luke 18:9–14 or 1 Corinthians 4:6–13.

When you lack faith in God, read Matthew 17:19–21, Mark 4:35–40, or Mark 11:20–23.

When you want to thank God, read Psalm 116, Psalm 118, or Luke 17:11–19.

When you need God's help, read Psalm 25 or Psalm 86.

When you feel alone, read Ephesians 4:1–16.

When _____,
read _____.

Appendix II

Raising Your Heart and Mind

Sign of the Cross

In the name of the Father,
and of the Son,
and of the Holy Spirit.
Amen.

The Lord's Prayer

Our Father, who art in heaven,
hallowed be your name;
your kingdom come;
your will be done on earth
as it is in heaven.
Give us this day our daily bread;
and forgive us our trespasses
as we forgive those
who trespass against us;
and lead us not into temptation,
but deliver us from evil. Amen.

Hail Mary

Hail, Mary, full of grace, the Lord is with you!
Blessed are you among women, and blessed
is the fruit of your womb, Jesus.
Holy Mary, Mother of God, pray for us
sinners, now and at the hour of our death.
Amen.

Trinity Prayer

Glory to the Father,
and to the Son,
and to the Holy Spirit.
As it was in the beginning, is now,
and will be forever. Amen.

Act of Contrition

O my God, I am sorry for my sins.
In choosing to sin and failing to do good,
I have sinned against you and your Church.
I firmly intend, with the help of your Son,
to do penance and to sin no more. Amen.

Serenity Prayer

O God, grant me the serenity to accept the things I
cannot change, the courage to change the things I can,
and the wisdom to know the difference.

Señal de la Cruz

En el nombre del Padre
y del Hijo
y del Espíritu Santo.
Amén.

Padre Nuestro

Padre nuestro, que estás en el cielo,
santificado sea to nombre;
venga tu reino;
hágase tu voluntad en el tierrs
como en el cielo.
Danos hay nuestro pan de cade día;
perdona nuestras ofensas como también
nosotros perdonamos a los que nos ofenden;
no nos dejes caer en tentación,
y líbranos del mal. Amén.

Ave Maria

Dios te salve, María, llena eres de gracia,
el Señor es contigo,
bendita Tú eres entre todas las mujeres,
y bendito es el fruto de tu vientre, Jesús.
Santa María, Madre de Dios,
ruéga por nosotros pecadores,
ahora y en la hora de nuestra muerte.
Amén.

Gloria

Gloria al Padre y al Hijo y al Espíritu Santo.
Como era en el principio ahora y siempre
por los siglos de los siglos. Amén.

Novena in Honor of the Immaculate Conception of the Blessed Virgin Mary

Almighty Father,
we offer this novena to honor the Blessed Virgin Mary.
She occupies a place in the Church which is highest
after Christ
and yet very close to us
for you chose her to give the world
that very Life which renews all things,
Jesus Christ, your Son and our Lord.
And so we praise you, Mary, virgin and mother.
After the Savior himself, you alone are all holy,
free from the stain of sin,
gifted by God from the first instant of your conception
with a unique holiness.
We praise and honor you.

Mary, free from all sin and led by the Holy Spirit,
you embraced God's saving will with a full heart,
and devoted yourself totally as a handmaid of the Lord
to the fulfillment of his will in your life,
and to the mystery of our redemption.
We thank you and love you.
Mary, your privileged and grace-filled origin
is the Father's final step in preparing humanity
to receive its Redeemer in human form.
Your fullness of grace is the Father's sign of his favor
to the Church
and also his promise to the Church
of its perfection as the Bride of Christ,
radiant in beauty.
Your holiness in the beginning of your life
is the foreshadowing of that all-embracing holiness
with which the Father will surround his people
when his Son comes at the end of time to greet us.
We bless you among all women.
Mary, we turn with confidence to you,
who are always ready to listen with a mother's affection
and powerful assistance.
Consoler of the afflicted,
Health of the sick,
Refuge of sinners,
grant us comfort in tribulation,
relief in sickness,
and liberating strength in our weakness.
You who are free from sin, lead us to combat sin.
Obtain for us the victory of hope over anguish,
of joy and beauty over boredom and disgust,
of eternal visions over temporal ones,
of life over death.
Mary, conceived without sin,
pray for us who have recourse to you.
(Individual petitions are mentioned here)
God our Father,
we make these petitions through Mary.
We pray most especially for the coming of your kingdom.
May you, together with your Son and the Holy Spirit,
be known, loved and glorified
and your law of love faithfully followed.
We pray in faith through Jesus Christ, your Son and
*   our Lord,*
in whom all fullness dwells,
now and for ever. Amen.

The Rosary

The Joyful Mysteries

1. The annunciation
2. The visitation
3. The birth of Jesus
4. The presentation in the temple
5. Mary and Joseph find Jesus in the temple

The Sorrowful Mysteries

1. The agony in the garden
2. The scourging of Jesus
3. The crowning with thorns
4. Jesus carries his cross
5. Jesus dies on the cross

The Glorious Mysteries

1. The resurrection
2. The ascension
3. The Holy Spirit is sent upon the apostles
4. The assumption of Mary
5. Mary is crowned queen of heaven and earth

Scriptural Stations of the Cross

First Station: Jesus prays in the Garden of Olives.

Second Station: Jesus is betrayed by Judas and arrested.

Third Station: Jesus is condemned by the Sanhedrin.

Fourth Station: Jesus is denied by Peter.

Fifth Station: Jesus is condemned by Pontius Pilate.

Sixth Station: Jesus is scourged and crowned with thorns.

Seventh Station: Jesus is made to carry the cross.

Eighth Station: Simon of Cyrene helps Jesus.

Ninth Station: Jesus meets the women of Jerusalem.

Tenth Station: Jesus is crucified.

Eleventh Station: Jesus promises the kingdom to the thief who repents.

Twelfth Station: Jesus speaks to his Mother and his friend John.

Thirteenth Station: Jesus dies on the cross.

Fourteenth Station: Jesus is laid in the tomb.

Dear Lord,
I want to take time out of this busy day to thank you for the many wonders you have given me. Please help me to overcome all the obstacles I face daily. Help me through this day, and forgive me for all of my faults. Amen.

—Jill Dunkel, age 16

I look to you, Lord, in times of emptiness
to satisfy my heart yearning for love.
I pray you will watch over me
as you hover in heaven above.
I ask for your comfort
on my darkest, saddest days,
And I know you'll guide me home
when all others have led me astray.
I thank you for always being there
even when I doubted you.
I know now and always you believe in me
and will forever see me through.
Most of all I know my faith
can only grow stronger,
As my days come closer to living with you
eternally and hopefully longer.

—Tera Bockenstedt, age 18

Prayer on Violence

In a world with so many pressures and temptations,
please give us the strength to trust in you to get through.
There are many people who turn to violence.
They think shooting,
killing,
stealing,
hurting
are the only things they can do.
Help them to see that if they turn to you,
we can make this world better.
A place to live,
love,
laugh.
The things God put us here to do.

—Kelly Boeckenstedt, age 16

Dear God,
Please bless all the people that have lost someone they love. It would really mean a lot to me if you would answer my prayer because I lost my dad two years ago. So God, would you please answer my prayer even though you have to answer millions a day?

—Luke Domeyer, age 12

Lord—
Some people say, "You only listen to those who pray" or "You love only those who are wealthy," but I know that is not true. Because only you could love every person created. It is with this spirit of faith and love that I ask for the gifts of health for the ill and disabled, faith for the unbelievers, guidance for those who lead and teach, comfort for those who mourn, forgiveness for those who have been wronged, hope for those in despair, and the gift of peace and love in the hearts of all humankind. Amen.

—Margene Deutmeyer, age 13

In Thanks for My Grandpa

My grandpa took me up in his plane
To see the beautiful land.
I felt free like a bird
And Grandpa took my hand.
He told me about his life
And how he always wanted to fly.
He didn't get to for the longest time.
Now how the time goes by.
Whenever he wants to get away,
He just takes his plane up in the air.
It's a good place for him to think
And God can hear him there.
Then he asks me what I want to be,
And I replied, "Just like you."
Then Grandpa asked me why,
And I said, "Because I want to fly, too."
Grandpa then landed on the runway
And gave the throttle a tug.
I then got out of the plane
And gave Grandpa a hug.

—Kristie Mormann, age 13